Professional Resumes Series

RESUMES FOR SOCIAL SERVICE CAREERS

The Editors of

VGM Career Horizons

Printed on recyclable paper

 **VGM Career Horizons**
a division of *NTC Publishing Group*
Lincolnwood, Illinois USA

Library of Congress Cataloging-in-Publication Data

Resumes for social service careers / The editors of VGM Career
Horizons.

   p. cm.
   ISBN 0–8442-4386-8 (soft)
   1. Human services—Vocational guidance.   2. Résumés (Employment)
I. Title.
HV 10.5.V49   1995   94-12516
361′.0023′73—dc20   CIP

Published by VGM Career Horizons, a division of NTC Publishing Group.
©1995 by NTC Publishing Group, 4255 West Touhy Avenue,
Lincolnwood (Chicago), Illinois 60646-1975, U.S.A.
Manufactured in the United States of America.

4 5 6 7 8 9 0 VP 9 8 7 6 5 4 3 2 1

ACKNOWLEDGMENT

The editors gratefully acknowledge Kathy Siebel for her help in the writing and production of this book.

CONTENTS

Introduction

Your resume is your first impression on a prospective employer. Though you may be articulate, intelligent, and charming in person, a poor resume may prevent you from ever having the opportunity to demonstrate your interpersonal skills, because a poor resume may prevent you from ever being called for an interview. While few people have ever been hired solely on the basis of their resume, a well-written, well-organized resume can go a long way toward helping you land an interview. Your resume's main purpose is to get you that interview. The rest is up to you and the employer. If you both feel that you are right for the job and the job is right for you, chances are you will be hired.

A resume must catch the reader's attention yet still be easy to read and to the point. Resume styles have changed over the years. Today, brief and focused resumes are preferred. No longer do employers have the patience, or the time, to review several pages of solid type. A resume should be only one page long, if possible, and never more than two pages. Time is a precious commodity in today's business world and the resume that is concise and straightforward will usually be the one that gets noticed.

Let's not make the mistake, though, of assuming that writing a brief resume means that you can take less care in preparing it. A successful resume takes time and thought, and if you are willing to make the effort, the rewards are well worth it. Think of your resume as a sales tool with the product being you. You want to sell yourself to a prospective employer. This book is designed to help you prepare a resume that will help you further your career—to land that next job, or first job, or to return to the work force after years of absence. So, read on. Make the effort and reap the rewards that a strong resume can bring to your career. Let's get to it!

Chapter One

THE ELEMENTS OF A GOOD RESUME

A winning resume is made of the elements that employers are most interested in seeing when reviewing a job applicant. These basic elements are the essential ingredients of a successful resume and become the actual sections of your resume. The following is a list of elements that may be used in a resume. Some are essential; some are optional. We will be discussing these in this chapter in order to give you a better understanding of each element's role in the makeup of your resume:

1. Heading
2. Objective
3. Work Experience
4. Education
5. Honors
6. Activities
7. Certificates and Licenses
8. Professional Memberships
9. Special Skills
10. Personal Information
11. References

The first step in preparing your resume is to gather together information about yourself and your past accomplishments. Later you will refine this information, rewrite it in the most effective language, and organize it into the most attractive layout. First, let's take a look at each of these important elements individually.

Heading

The heading may seem to be a simple enough element in your resume, but be careful not to take it lightly. The heading should be placed at the top of your resume and should include your name, home address, and telephone numbers. If you can take calls at your current place of business, include your business number, since most employers will attempt to contact you during the business day. If this is not possible, or if you can afford it, purchase an answering machine that allows you to retrieve your messages while you are away from home. This way you can make sure you don't miss important phone calls. *Always* include your phone number on your resume. It is crucial that when prospective employers need to have immediate contact with you, they can.

Objective

When seeking a particular career path, it is important to list a job objective on your resume. This statement helps employers know the direction that you see yourself heading, so that they can determine whether your goals are in line with the position available. The objective is normally one sentence long and describes your employment goals clearly and concisely. See the sample resumes in this book for examples of objective statements.

The job objective will vary depending on the type of person you are, the field you are in, and the type of goals you have. It can be either specific or general, but it should always be to the point.

In some cases, this element is not necessary, but usually it is a good idea to include your objective. It gives your possible future employer an idea of where you are coming from and where you want to go.

The objective statement is better left out, however, if you are uncertain of the exact title of the job you seek. In such a case, the inclusion of an overly specific objective statement could result in your not being considered for a variety of acceptable positions; you should be sure to incorporate this information in your cover letter, instead.

Work Experience

This element is arguably the most important of them all. It will provide the central focus of your resume, so it is necessary that this section be as complete as possible. Only by examining your work experience in depth can you get to the heart of your accomplishments and present them in a way that demonstrates the strength of your qualifications. Of course, someone just out of school will have less work experience than someone who has been working for a number of years, but the amount of information isn't the most important thing—rather, how it is presented and how it highlights you as a person and as a worker will be what counts.

As you work on this section of your resume, be aware of the need for accuracy. You'll want to include all necessary information about each of your jobs, including job title, dates, employer, city, state, responsibilities, special projects, and accomplishments. Be sure to only list company accomplishments for which you were directly responsible. If you haven't participated in any special projects, that's all right—this area may not be relevant to certain jobs.

The most common way to list your work experience is in *reverse chronological order*. In other words, start with your most recent job and work your way backwards. This way your prospective employer sees your current (and often most important) job before seeing your past jobs. Your most recent position, if the most important, should also be the one that includes the most information, as compared to your previous positions. If you are just out of school, show your summer employment and part-time work, though in this case your education will most likely be more important than your work experience.

The following worksheets will help you gather information about your past jobs.

WORK EXPERIENCE
Job One:

Job Title _____

Dates _____

Employer _____

City, State _____

Major Duties _____

_____

_____

_____

_____

_____

_____

_____

_____

Special Projects _____

_____

_____

_____

Accomplishments _____

_____

_____

_____

_____

_____

_____

_____

Job Two:

Job Title _____

Dates _____

Employer _____

City, State _____

Major Duties _____

_____

_____

_____

_____

_____

_____

_____

Special Projects _____

_____

_____

_____

Accomplishments _____

_____

_____

_____

_____

_____

_____

_____

_____

Job Three:

Job Title _____

Dates _____

Employer _____

City, State _____

Major Duties _____

_____

_____

_____

_____

_____

_____

_____

_____

Special Projects _____

_____

_____

_____

Accomplishments _____

_____

_____

_____

_____

_____

_____

_____

_____

Job Four:

Job Title _____

Dates _____

Employer _____

City, State _____

Major Duties _____

_____

_____

_____

_____

_____

_____

_____

Special Projects _____

_____

_____

_____

Accomplishments _____

_____

_____

_____

_____

_____

_____

_____

_____

Education

Education is the second most important element of a resume. Your educational background is often a deciding factor in an employer's decision to hire you. Be sure to stress your accomplishments in school with the same finesse that you stressed your accomplishments at work. If you are looking for your first job, your education will be your greatest asset, since your work experience will most likely be minimal. In this case, the education section becomes the most important. You will want to be sure to include any degrees or certificates you received, your major area of concentration, any honors, and any relevant activities. Again, be sure to list your most recent schooling first. If you have completed graduate-level work, begin with that and work in reverse chronological order through your undergraduate education. If you have completed an undergraduate degree, you may choose whether to list your high school experience or not. This should be done only if your high school grade-point average was well above average.

The following worksheets will help you gather information for this section of your resume. Also included are supplemental worksheets for honors and for activities. Sometimes honors and activities are listed in a section separate from education, most often near the end of the resume.

EDUCATION

School _____

Major or Area of Concentration _____

Degree _____

Date _____

School _____

Major or Area of Concentration _____

Degree _____

Date _____

Honors

Here, you should list any awards, honors, or memberships in honorary societies that you have received. Usually these are of an academic nature, but they can also be for special achievement in sports, clubs, or other school activities. Always be sure to include the name of the organization honoring you and the date(s) received. Use the worksheet below to help gather your honors information.

HONORS

Honor: _____

Awarding Organization: _____

Date(s): _____

Honor: _____

Awarding Organization: _____

Date(s): _____

Honor: _____

Awarding Organization: _____

Date(s): _____

Honor: _____

Awarding Organization: _____

Date(s): _____

Activities

You may have been active in different organizations or clubs during your years at school; often an employer will look at such involvement as evidence of initiative and dedication. Your ability to take an active role, and even a leadership role, in a group should be included on your resume. Use the worksheet provided to list your activities and accomplishments in this area. In general, you should exclude any organization the name of which indicates the race, creed, sex, age, marital status, color, or nation of origin of its members.

ACTIVITIES

Organization/Activity: _____

Accomplishments: _____

_____

_____

Organization/Activity: _____

Accomplishments: _____

_____

_____

Organization/Activity: _____

Accomplishments: _____

_____

_____

Organization/Activity: _____

Accomplishments: _____

_____

_____

As your work experience increases through the years, your school activities and honors will play less of a role in your resume, and eventually you will most likely only list your degree and any major honors you received. This is due to the fact that, as time goes by, your job performance becomes the most important element in your resume. Through time, your resume should change to reflect this.

Certificates and Licenses

The next potential element of your resume is certificates and licenses. You should list these if the job you are seeking requires them and you, of course, have acquired them. If you have applied for a license, but have not yet received it, use the phrase "application pending."

License requirements vary by state. If you have moved or you are planning to move to another state, be sure to check with the appropriate board or licensing agency in the state in which you are applying for work to be sure that you are aware of all licensing requirements.

Always be sure that all of the information you list is completely accurate. Locate copies of your licenses and certificates and check the exact date and name of the accrediting agency. Use the following worksheet to list your licenses and certificates. .

CERTIFICATES AND LICENSES

Name of License: _____

Licensing Agency: _____

Date Issued: _____

Name of License: _____

Licensing Agency: _____

Date Issued: _____

Name of License: _____

Licensing Agency: _____

Date Issued: _____

Professional Memberships

Another potential element in your resume is a section listing professional memberships. Use this section to list involvement in professional associations, unions, and similar organizations. It is to your advantage to list any professional memberships that pertain to the job you are seeking. Be sure to include the dates of your involvement and whether you took part in any special activities or held any offices within the organization. Use the following worksheet to gather your information.

PROFESSIONAL MEMBERSHIPS

Name of Organization: _____

Offices Held: _____

Activities: _____

Date(s): _____

Name of Organization: _____

Offices Held: _____

Activities: _____

Date(s): _____

Name of Organization: _____

Offices Held: _____

Activities: _____

Date(s): _____

Name of Organization: _____

Offices Held: _____

Activities: _____

Date(s): _____

Special Skills

This section of your resume is set aside for mentioning any special abilities you have that could relate to the job you are seeking. This is the part of your resume where you have the opportunity to demonstrate certain talents and experiences that are not necessarily a part of your educational or work experience. Common examples include fluency in a foreign language, or knowledge of a particular computer application.

Special skills can encompass a wide range of your talents—remember to be sure that whatever skills you list relate to the type of work you are looking for.

Personal Information

Some people include "Personal" information on their resumes. This is not generally recommended, but you might wish to include it if you think that something in your personal life, such as a hobby or talent, has some bearing on the position you are seeking. This type of information is often referred to at the beginning of an interview, when it is used as an "ice breaker." Of course, personal information regarding age, marital status, race, religion, or sexual preference should never appear on any resume.

References

References are not usually listed on the resume, but a prospective employer needs to know that you have references who may be contacted if necessary. All that is necessary to include in your resume regarding references is a sentence at the bottom stating, "References are available upon request." If a prospective employer requests a list of references, be sure to have one ready. Also, check with whomever you list to see if it is all right for you to use them as a reference. Forewarn them that they may receive a call regarding a reference for you. This way they can be prepared to give you the best reference possible.

Chapter Two

WRITING YOUR RESUME

*N*ow that you have gathered together all of the information for each of the sections of your resume, it's time to write out each section in a way that will get the attention of whoever is reviewing it. The type of language you use in your resume will affect its success. You want to take the information you have gathered and translate it into a language that will cause a potential employer to sit up and take notice.

Resume writing is not like expository writing or creative writing. It embodies a functional, direct writing style and focuses on the use of action words. By using action words in your writing, you more effectively stress past accomplishments. Action words help demonstrate your initiative and highlight your talents. Always use verbs that show strength and reflect the qualities of a "doer." By using action words, you characterize yourself as a person who takes action, and this will impress potential employers.

The following is a list of verbs commonly used in resume writing. Use this list to choose the action words that can help your resume become a strong one:

administered	introduced
advised	invented
analyzed	maintained
arranged	managed
assembled	met with
assumed responsibility	motivated
billed	negotiated
built	operated
carried out	orchestrated
channeled	ordered
collected	organized
communicated	oversaw
compiled	performed
completed	planned
conducted	prepared
contacted	presented
contracted	produced
coordinated	programmed
counseled	published
created	purchased
cut	recommended
designed	recorded
determined	reduced
developed	referred
directed	represented
dispatched	researched
distributed	reviewed
documented	saved
edited	screened
established	served as
expanded	served on
functioned as	sold
gathered	suggested
handled	supervised
hired	taught
implemented	tested
improved	trained
inspected	typed
interviewed	wrote

Now take a look at the information you put down on the work experience worksheets. Take that information and rewrite it in paragraph form, using verbs to highlight your actions and accomplishments. Let's look at an example, remembering that what matters here is the writing style, and not the particular job responsibilities given in our sample.

WORK EXPERIENCE
Regional Sales Manager

Manager of sales representatives from seven states. Responsible for twelve food chain accounts in the East. In charge of directing the sales force in planned selling toward specific goals. Supervisor and trainer of new sales representatives. Consulting for customers in the areas of inventory management and quality control.

Special Projects: Coordinator and sponsor of annual food industry sales seminar.

Accomplishments: Monthly regional volume went up 25 percent during my tenure while, at the same time, a proper sales/cost ratio was maintained. Customer/company relations improved significantly.

Below is the rewritten version of this information, using action words. Notice how much stronger it sounds.

WORK EXPERIENCE
Regional Sales Manager

Managed sales representatives from seven states. Handled twelve food chain accounts in the eastern United States. Directed the sales force in planned selling towards specific goals. Supervised and trained new sales representatives. Consulted for customers in the areas of inventory management and quality control. Coordinated and sponsored the annual Food Industry Seminar. Increased monthly regional volume 25 percent and helped to improve customer/company relations during my tenure.

Another way of constructing the work experience section is by using actual job descriptions. Job descriptions are rarely written using the proper resume language, but they do include all the information necessary to create this section of your resume. Take the description of one of the jobs your are including on your resume (if you have access to it), and turn it into an action-oriented paragraph. Below is an example of a job description followed by a version of the same description written using action words. Again, pay attention to the style of writing, as the details of your own work experience will be unique.

PUBLIC ADMINISTRATOR I

Responsibilities: Coordinate and direct public services to meet the needs of the nation, state, or community. Analyze problems; work with special committees and public agencies; recommend solutions to governing bodies.

Aptitudes and Skills: Ability to relate to and communicate with people; solve complex problems through analysis; plan, organize, and implement policies and programs. Knowledge of political systems; financial management; personnel administration; program evaluation; organizational theory.

WORK EXPERIENCE
Public Administrator I

Wrote pamphlets and conducted discussion groups to inform citizens of legislative processes and consumer issues. Organized and supervised 25 interviewers. Trained interviewers in effective communication skills.

Now that you have learned how to word your resume, you are ready for the next step in your quest for a winning resume: assembly and layout.

Chapter Three

ASSEMBLY AND LAYOUT

*A*t this point, you've gathered all the necessary information for your resume, and you've rewritten it using the language necessary to impress potential employers. Your next step is to assemble these elements in a logical order and then to lay them out on the page neatly and attractively in order to achieve the desired effect: getting that interview.

Assembly

The order of the elements in a resume makes a difference in its overall effect. Obviously, you would not want to put your name and address in the middle of the resume or your special skills section at the top. You want to put the elements in an order that stresses your most important achievements, not the less pertinent information. For example, if you recently graduated from school and have no full-time work experience, you will want to list your education before you list any part-time jobs you may have held during school. On the other hand, if you have been gainfully employed for several years and currently hold an important position in your company, you will want to list your work experience ahead of your education, which has become less pertinent with time.

There are some elements that are always included in your resume and some that are optional. Following is a list of essential and optional elements:

Essential	*Optional*
Name	Job Objective
Address	Honors
Phone Number	Special Skills
Work Experience	Professional Memberships
Education	Activities
References Phrase	Certificates and Licenses
	Personal Information

Your choice of optional sections depends on your own background and employment needs. Always use information that will put you and your abilities in a favorable light. If your honors are impressive, then be sure to include them in your resume. If your activities in school demonstrate particular talents necessary for the job you are seeking, then allow space for a section on activities. Each resume is unique, just as each person is unique.

Types of Resumes

So far, our discussion about resumes has involved the most common type—the *reverse chronological* resume, in which your most recent job is listed first and so on. This is the type of resume usually preferred by human resources directors, and it is the one most frequently used. However, in some cases this style of presentation is not the most effective way to highlight your skills and accomplishments.

For someone reentering the work force after many years or someone looking to change career fields, the *functional resume* may work best. This type of resume focuses more on achievement and less on the sequence of your work history. In the functional resume, your experience is presented by what you have accomplished and the skills you have developed in your past work.

A functional resume can be assembled from the same information you collected for your chronological resume. The main difference lies in how you organize this information. Essentially, the work experience section becomes two sections, with your job duties and accomplishments comprising one section and your employer's name, city, state, your position, and the dates employed making up another section. The first section is placed near the top of the resume, just below the job objective section, and can be called *Accomplishments* or *Achievements*. The second section, containing the bare essentials of your employment history, should come after the accomplishments section and can be titled *Work Experience* or *Employment History*. The other sections of your resume remain the same. The work experience section is the only one affected in the functional resume. By placing the section that focuses on your achievements first, you thereby draw attention to these achievements. This puts less emphasis on who you worked for and more emphasis on what you did and what you are capable of doing.

For someone changing careers, emphasis on skills and achievements is essential. The identities of previous employers, which may be unrelated to one's new job field, need to be downplayed. The functional resume accomplishes this task. For someone reentering the work force after many years, a functional resume is the obvious choice. If you lack full-time work experience, you will need to draw attention away from this fact and instead focus on your skills and abilities gained possibly through volunteer activities or part-time work. Education may also play a more important role in this resume.

Which type of resume is right for you will depend on your own personal circumstances. It may be helpful to create a chronological *and* a functional resume and then compare the two to find out which is more suitable. The sample resumes found in this book include both chronological and functional resumes. Use these resumes as guides to help you decide on the content and appearance of your own resume.

Layout

Once you have decided which elements to include in your resume and you have arranged them in an order that makes sense and emphasizes your achievements and abilities, then it is time to work on the physical layout of your resume.

There is no single appropriate layout that applies to every resume, but there are a few basic rules to follow in putting your resume on paper:

1. Leave a comfortable margin on the sides, top, and bottom of the page (usually 1 to 1½ inches).

2. Use appropriate spacing between the sections (usually 2 to 3 line spaces are adequate).

3. Be consistent in the *type* of headings you use for the different sections of your resume. For example, if you capitalize the heading EMPLOYMENT HISTORY, don't use initial capitals and underlining for a heading of equal importance, such as Education.

4. Always try to fit your resume onto one page. If you are having trouble fitting all your information onto one page, perhaps you are trying to say too much. Try to edit out any repetitive or unnecessary information or possibly shorten descriptions of earlier jobs. Be ruthless. Maybe you've included too many optional sections.

CHRONOLOGICAL RESUME

Roger Boyd
673 Drake Street
Pittsburgh, PA 15234
Phone: 412-555-6453

Job Objective:

A legal position with a social service agency

Employment:

1993-Present   **District Attorney's Office, Pittsburgh**
Assistant District Attorney
Criminal Courts Division

Take depositions from witnesses and complaintants.
Prepare cases for trial: legal research and writing,
filing of motions.

1990-1993   **Morgan & Ryan Legal Corporation, Pittsburgh**
Law Clerk

Interviewed clients for attorneys.
Filed court documents.
Standardized manual office procedures and fully
computerized office.

1988-1990   **Warren County Department of Social Services**
Warren, PA
Caseworker II

Established family eligibility for food stamps, public aid,
medicare, and other programs. Maintained average
caseload of 75-125 clients at a time.

Education:

B.A. in Sociology, University of Pittsburgh
J.D. Northwestern University, Chicago, IL

References Available Upon Request

FUNCTIONAL RESUME

Catherine Walker
664 Prospect Avenue
Dover, Delaware 19901
(606) 555-5346

Objective: To obtain a position as a special education assistant in
a school or residential setting.

Skills: Team teaching
Tutoring
Nursing assistance
Understanding of emotional, behavioral & learning disabilities
Fluent in Spanish

Education: 1993, B.A. in Sociology, Delaware State College
Coursework in Special Education at Delaware State, part-time,
working toward an M.A. in Special education

Member of New England chapter of Association for Children and Adults
with Learning Disabilities

**Work
History:** Staff Assistant , 1994-Present, Gateway Services

Aid professional staff of this residential program for handicapped adults.
Assist in providing educational services, occupational therapy,
and nursing services.

Teacher's Assistant, 1993-1994, Elementary School District 58

Classroom experience with students affected by emotional & behavioral
difficulties, and learning disabilities. Assisted in preparation and
implementation of individualized lesson plans for students. Provided
progress reports to teacher, parents, and school psychologist.

References Available on Request

Don't let the idea of having to tell every detail about your life get in the way of producing a resume that is simple and straightforward. The more compact your resume, the easier it will be to read and the better an impression it will make for you.

In some cases, the resume will not fit on a single page, even after extensive editing. In such cases, the resume should be printed on two pages so as not to compromise clarity or appearance. Each page of a two-page resume should be marked clearly with your name and the page number, e.g., "Judith Ramirez, page 1 of 2." The pages should then be stapled together.

Try experimenting with various layouts until you find one that looks good to you. Always show your final layout to other people and ask them what they like or dislike about it, and what impresses them most about your resume. Make sure that is what you want most to emphasize. If it isn't, you may want to consider making changes in your layout until the necessary information is emphasized. Use the sample resumes in this book to get some ideas for laying out your resume.

Putting Your Resume in Print

Your resume should be typed or printed on good quality 8½″ × 11″ bond paper. You want to make as good an impression as possible with your resume; therefore, quality paper is a necessity. If you have access to a word processor with a good printer, or know of someone who does, make use of it. Typewritten resumes should only be used when there are no other options available.

After you have produced a clean original, you will want to make duplicate copies of it. Usually a copy shop is your best bet for producing copies without smudges or streaks. Make sure you have the copy shop use quality bond paper for all copies of your resume. Ask for a sample copy before they run your entire order. After copies are made, check each copy for cleanliness and clarity.

Another more costly option is to have your resume typeset and printed by a printer. This will provide the most attractive resume of all. If you anticipate needing a lot of copies of your resume, the cost of having it typeset may be justified.

Proofreading

After you have finished typing the master copy of your resume and before you go to have it copied or printed, you must thoroughly check it for typing and spelling errors. Have several people read it over just in case you may have missed an error. Misspelled words and typing mistakes will not make a good impression on a prospective employer, as they are a bad reflection on your writing ability and your attention to detail. With thorough and conscientious proofreading, these mistakes can be avoided.

The following are some rules of capitalization and punctuation that may come in handy when proofreading your resume:

Rules of Capitalization

- Capitalize proper nouns, such as names of schools, colleges, and universities, names of companies, and brand names of products.

- Capitalize major words in the names and titles of books, tests, and articles that appear in the body of your resume.

- Capitalize words in major section headings of your resume.

- Do not capitalize words just because they seem important.

- When in doubt, consult a manual of style such as *Words Into Type* (Prentice-Hall), or *The Chicago Manual of Style* (The University of Chicago Press). Your local library can help you locate these and other reference books.

Rules of Punctuation

- Use a comma to separate words in a series.

- Use a semicolon to separate series of words that already include commas within the series.

- Use a semicolon to separate independent clauses that are not joined by a conjunction.

- Use a period to end a sentence.

- Use a colon to show that the examples or details that follow expand or amplify the preceding phrase.

- Avoid the use of dashes.

- Avoid the use of brackets.

- If you use any punctuation in an unusual way in your resume, be consistent in its use.

- Whenever you are uncertain, consult a style manual.

Chapter Four

THE COVER LETTER

*O*nce your resume has been assembled, laid out, and printed to your satisfaction, the next and final step before distribution is to write your cover letter. Though there may be instances where you deliver your resume in person, most often you will be sending it through the mail. Resumes sent through the mail always need an accompanying letter that briefly introduces you and your resume. The purpose of the cover letter is to get a potential employer to read your resume, just as the purpose of your resume is to get that same potential employer to call you for an interview.

Like your resume, your cover letter should be clean, neat, and direct. A cover letter usually includes the following information:

1. Your name and address.

2. The date.

3. The name and address of the person and company to whom you are sending your resume.

4. The salutation ("Dear Mr." or "Dear Ms." followed by the person's last name, or "To Whom It May Concern").

5. An opening paragraph explaining why you are writing (in response to an ad, the result of a previous meeting, at the suggestion of someone you both know) and indicating your interest in the job being offered.

6. One or two more paragraphs that tell why you want to work for the company and what qualifications and experience you can bring to that company.

7. A final paragraph that closes the letter and requests that you be contacted for an interview. You may mention here that your references are available upon request.

8. The closing ("Sincerely," or "Yours Truly," followed by your signature with your name typed under it).

Your cover letter, including all of the information above, should be no more than one page in length. The language used should be polite, businesslike, and to the point. Do not attempt to tell your life story in the cover letter. A long and cluttered letter will only serve to put off the reader. Remember, you only need to mention a few of your accomplishments and skills in the cover letter. The rest of your information is in your resume. Each and every achievement should not be mentioned twice. If your cover letter is a success, your resume will be read and all pertinent information reviewed by your prospective employer.

Producing the Cover Letter

Cover letters should always be typed individually, since they are always written to particular individuals and companies. Never use a form letter for your cover letter. Each one should be as personal as possible. Of course, once you have written and rewritten your first cover letter to the point where you are satisfied with it, you certainly can use similar wording in subsequent letters.

After you have typed your cover letter on quality bond paper, be sure to proofread it as thoroughly as you did your resume. Again, spelling errors are a sure sign of carelessness, and you don't want that to be a part of your first impression on a prospective employer. Make sure to handle the letter and resume carefully to avoid any smudges, and then mail both your cover letter and resume in an appropriate sized envelope. Be sure to keep an accurate record of all the resumes you send out and the results of each mailing.

Numerous sample cover letters appear at the end of the book. Use them as models for your own cover letter or to get an idea of how cover letters are put together. Remember, every one is unique and depends on the particular circumstances of the individual writing it and the job for which he or she is applying.

About a week after mailing resumes and cover letters to potential employers, you will want to contact them by telephone. Confirm that your resume arrived, and ask whether an interview might be possible. Getting your foot in the door during this call is half the battle of a job search, and a strong resume and cover letter will help you immeasurably.

Chapter Five

SAMPLE RESUMES

This chapter contains dozens of sample resumes for people pursuing a wide variety of jobs and careers within this field.

There are many different styles of resumes in terms of graphic layout and presentation of information. These samples also represent people with varying amounts of education and work experience. Use these samples to model your own resume after. Choose one resume, or borrow elements from several different resumes to help you construct your own.

Jane Fitzgerald
208 Prince George Street
Annapolis, MD 21401
(301) 268-1799

EDUCATION

George Washington University, Washington, D.C. M.A. Art Therapy, 1983.

Stockton State College, Pomona, NJ. B.A. Art, Psychology minor, 1979.

EXPERIENCE

Center for Children, Inc., La Plata, MD. Individual and group therapist for victims of sexual abuse and their families. Initiated and supervised art therapy program for atonements with eating disorders. January 1991-Present.

Anne Arundel County Department of Social Services, Anne Arundel, MD. Individual and group therapist for sexually and physically abused children. Facilitator of staff enrichment group. November, 1987-December, 1990.

Charter Hospital, Charlottesville, VA. Provided art therapy to psychiatric patients in individual and group sessions. Served as treatment team member on the adult unit. Field supervisor for master level interns. Staff enrichment coordinator. March 1984-September 1987.

Department of Human Services, Washington, D.C. Assisted social worker with cases involving abused and neglected children. Responsibilities included counseling, field and family visits, and preparing materials for court hearings. November 1983-March 1984.

The Joseph P. Kennedy Institute, Washington, D.C. Art therapist intern for developmentally disabled students ages 5-12. George Washington University Medical Center Psychiatric Unit. Worked with hyperactive children, Alzheimer's patients, and anorectics. September 1981-May 1982.

The Helmbold Education Center for the Mentally Handicapped, Ventnor, NJ. Psychology Intern. January 1979-June, 1981.

Jane Fitzgerald page 1 of 2

Department of Continuing Education, Stocton State College, Pomona, NJ. Adjunct Instructor of Art. June, 1978-May, 1979.

PRESENTATIONS   "Abuse Prevention-for Children." U.S. Naval Academy, MD. February 1993.

"A Special Blend: The Role of Creative Arts and Expressive Therapy." Annual meeting of the Associated Psychotherapists of Maryland. June 1991

"Stress Management for Older Adults." Senior Citizen's Center, Anne Arundel, MD. December 1990.

PUBLICATIONS   "Art Psychotherapy in the Treatment of the Chemically Dependent Patient." <u>Arts in Psychotherapy Journal</u>. Summer, 1989.

"Art Therapy: An Effective Strategy in the Counseling of Alzheimer's Patients." <u>Arts in Psychotherapy Journal</u>. Fall, 1990.

"Art Therapy and the Abused Child." <u>American Journal of Child and Adolescent Psychiatric Nursing</u>. August 1993.

<u>From My Heart to Yours.</u> Anticipated publication January 1995.

AFFILIATIONS   The American Art Therapy Association: Credentialed Professional Member.

References Available Upon Request

Carter M. Winslow
555 Amsterdam Avenue
New York, NY. 10024
(212) 555-5727

Professional Objective

To secure a position as a social worker with an agency that will enable me to apply my eight years of counseling and administrative experience.

Employment History

Institute for Behavior Resources, Washington, D.C. March 1992-present. Director of Youth Group Program for neglected and abused children. Responsible for staff of seven full time case workers and six volunteers including screening and training of new staff members. Program's liaison with community and state agencies. Prepared grant proposals which accounted for 70% of program's funding.

Institute for Behavior Resources, Washington, D.C. October 1988-March 1992. Youth Group Program social worker. Conducted psychosocial assessments and implemented appropriate counseling for neglected and abused children ages 7-12. Conducted workshops for educators and day care personnel on identifying signs of neglect and abuse and the proper procedure for reporting cases of suspected abuse. Served as consultant to State Child Welfare Department.

George Washington University Medical Center, Washington, D.C. June 1987-September 1988. Pediatric ward counselor. Led individual and group therapy sessions for children with physical injury related trauma. Counseled family members and designed and implemented support group for siblings of pediatric patients.

Family and Child Services, Washington. D.C. June 1986-May 1987. Social work intern. Collected statistical data on foster care placement of D.C. area children for annual report presented to the Mayor's Council.

Hope House, Washington, D.C. November 1984-May 1986. Volunteer counselor for children in safe house for battered women and their families.

Education

George Washington University, Washington, D.C. MSW, 1986
University of Maryland, College Park, MD. BA, Psychology, 1984.

References Available Upon Request

Sandra J. Hollis
24 Beech Hollow Lane
Gadsden, AL 35910
Home: (205)555-6629
Office: (205)555-7905

EXPERIENCE

Town Manager, Gadsden, AL.   1986-present
- Represent Gadsden in the transaction of its affairs with government agencies,
  community organizations, businesses, and town residents

- Supervise six department heads and provided for efficient delivery of financial,
  administrative, and other staff services

- Oversee the implementation and enforcement of ordinances and regulations

- Prepare and submit annual budget and manage town finances

- Make appropriate policy recommendations to Town Commissioners

- Coordinate municipal economic development policies

- Administer municipal elections and supervise voter registration

- Knowledgeable in infrastructure and development financing, zoning and subdivision
  practices, Community Development Block Grant regulations, property acquisitions,
  and procurement practices

Anniston Business Consultants, Birmingham, AL   1984-1986
- Consultant to county offices, providing information and advice on financial matters

- Conducted personnel finance seminars and consulted with individual clients

- Researched and wrote money management article for local newspaper

Business Instructor, Birmingham Community College, Birmingham, AL.
                                                                  1980-1984
- Responsible for instruction of four classes per semester

- Member of Business Education Committee, completed report containing
  recommendations for restructuring the college Business program

- Conducted mini-seminars on financial planning and investment for Seniors Program

Sandra J. Hollis page 1 of 2

History Teacher, Piedmont Middle School, Piedmont, AL.   1974-1978
  - Responsible for the instruction of five history courses, including curriculum
    development, presentation, and evaluation of student achievement

- Teacher Representative to Board of Education 1977-1978

  - Girls' basketball coach and assistant drama coach

EDUCATION

MBA, Alabama State University, 1979
BA, History, Smith College, 1974

References available upon request

Jonathan K. Sanders
6 Weybridge Place
Chapel Hill, NC 27514
(910) 555-3469

Career Objective
To obtain a counseling position with a non-profit organization that serves the needs of the homeless population.

Experience

1993-1995   Job Development Counselor, Job Find, Chapel Hill, NC.
- Provided job counseling to homeless men in three area transitional housing programs
- Increased community business participation in job placement program by 50%.
- Organized weekly employment workshops and quarterly job fairs
- Increased revenue for job training 30% through community fundraising and 25% through federal grants
- Wrote quarterly newsletter distributed to county businesses
- Provided training seminars to shelter staffers throughout North Carolina regarding effective job counseling strategies

1989-1993   Volunteer Hewlett Men's Shelter, Chapel Hill, NC.
- Responsible for overnight coverage of twelve bed facility two nights per week
- Member of committee for volunteer recruitment
- Chairperson fundraising committee
- Provided information regarding social services programs

Education

1993 University of North Carolina, Chapel Hill, B.A. Business

Anticipated MSW Spring 1996, Duke University

References

Provided Upon Request

Michael J. Cullings
P.O. Box 406
Sedona, Arizona 86336
(602) 555- 0926

Career Objective
A challenging position in speech therapy in which I have the opportunity to use my education and proven work experience to advance to an administrative position.

Work Experience

October 1992- present	***NovaCare, Flagstaff, AZ.*** Assistant co-ordinator of speech therapy. Responsibilities include assigning cases to staff members, evaluating progress of interdisciplinary rehabilitation team, training new personnel, and serving as patient advocate. Administered individual treatment to patients with non-birth-related speech impairments.
May 1988- July 1992	***Flagstaff Health Department, Flagstaff, AZ.*** Staff speech therapist. Administered diagnostic tests, interpreted data, and developed appropriate treatments for clients age 4 to 86. Supervised speech therapy interns.
April 1986- May 1988	***Ohio Public Schools, Columbus, OH*** . Speech therapist. Routine testing of school children. Individual and group therapist for first through sixth graders. Provided family support . Liaison between school and other community resources.
January 1985- November 1985	***Columbus Department of Social Services, Columbus, OH.*** Speech therapy intern. Assisted therapists in developing and implementing treatment. Responsible for diagnostic testing.
September 1983- December 1984	***Columbus Public Schools, Columbus, OH.*** Substitute teacher.

Education

1985	M.A. Speech Therapy. Ohio State University
1983	B.A. Education. Drew University

Certifications
Arizona State Licensed Speech Therapist
Certificate of Clinical Competence in Therapy

References Available Upon Request

Robert Martin
2108 Rusk Street
Beaumont, TX 77701
(409) 555-8740

Experience

Houston Correctional Center, Houston, TX. Correctional Specialist. Screen repeat juvenile offenders for potential placement in diversion programs. Assessment includes conducting interviews with offenders, reviewing police reports, interpreting psychological data, and conferring with other state appointed personnel. Determine appropriate diversion placement and monitor progress through visitations, interviews and follow up case reporting.   1989-present

Long Lane Center, Liberty, TX. Live-In Counselor. Provided overnight supervision for sixteen adolescent boys with history of juvenile delinquency. Provided individual and group alcohol and substance abuse counseling. Initiated after school work placement program and peer support groups. Worked in conjunction with Department of Children's Services and Houston Correctional Department.   1984-1988

Center Stage Youth Hotline, Houston, TX. Coordinator of volunteers. Supervised twenty-two volunteers for 24-hour youth hotline. Initiated after school and weekend peer counseling program.   1981-1988

Houston Police Department, Houston, TX. Police Officer. Specialized in juvenile cases. Conducted seminars for educators and parents on issue of alcohol and substance abuse. Served as law enforcement liaison to Children's Court Appointed Advocacy Program.   1979-1982

Education

1984   B.A. Psychology, Texas State University
1979   Graduate of Houston Police Academy

References Available Upon Request

Melinda F. Jarviss
S. Inland Empire Way
Spokane, WA 99204
(509) 555-2641

Career Objective: To obtain a position in which I can combine my teaching experience with my concern for the environment.

Work Experience

1993-present | *Environmental Education Group, Kettle Falls, WA.* Field Instructor. Provide environmental conservation education and appreciation to elementary school children. Lead school groups on nature hikes in and around Coulee Dam National Area. Prepare educational materials to supplement outdoor lessons. Visit local schools and prepare resource materials for classroom teachers.

1988-1993 | *Hanover Elementary School, Hanover, PA.* Fourth and fifth grade science teacher. Responsible for all aspects of classroom management and instruction including lesson planning, evaluation, and reporting. Initiated and supervised elementary science fair.

1987 | *Frederick Elementary School, Abbotstown, PA.* Student teacher. Responsible for the instruction of four elementary science classes.

Education
1987   B.S. Biology, Gettysburg College

Certifications
Washington State Board of Education Elementary Certification
Pennsylvania State Board of Education Master Educator, Elementary Certification

Memberships
Friends of Earth
Mt. Spokane Conservation Group
Spokane Recycling Committee
American Association of Environmental Educators

References Available Upon Request

James W. Mitchell

169 Schoolhouse Lane

Westbrook, CT 06498

Work: (203) 555-9422

Home: (203) 555-6421

EDUCATION

University of Connecticut, Stoors, CT. M.Ed. 1989. Secondary education with English as a Second Language concentration. 3.8 G.P.A.

Wesleyan University, Middletown, CT. B.A. 1984. English major, Spanish minor. Graduate of the Educational Studies Program.

WORK HISTORY

Middlesex County Board of Education, Middletown, CT.   May 1993-present
Co-ordinator of county ESL instruction. Revised ESL teacher training program. Initiated mandatory in-service programming for all county teachers regarding the instruction of non-English speaking and bilingual students. Administer diagnostic tests and interpret data. Supervise six county ESL instructors.

Shoreline Educational Institute, Old Saybrook, CT.   July 1990-present
ESL instructor for non-English speaking students including individual and group lessons. Consultant to Connecticut State Board of Education Special Education Department.

Guilford High School, Guilford, CT.   August 1986-June 1990
Planned and taught Spanish levels II and IV. Developed and supervised Spanish curriculum for elementary school enrichment program. Foreign Language Department Chairman, 1988-1990.

Morgan High School, Clinton, CT.   September 1984-June 1986
Secondary level Spanish teacher. Responsible for curriculum development and implementation. Introduced and advised school's Spanish club including international school exchanges.

CREDENTIALS

Connecticut Board of Education Certified Teacher

Association Member Connecticut ESL Instructors

American Association of ESL Instructors

References and additional information provided on request.

Drew B. Hopkins
14 Hayward Street
Yonkers, NY. 10704
Home: (718) 555-0190
Office: (917) 555-8172

Work Experience

1990-Present **Northeast Bankers Association, New York, NY.** Information Specialist. Responsible for answering ready-reference and servicing quality questions, completing in depth manual research, researching and writing monthly article for association magazine. Proficient in utilizing on-line data bases through DIALOG.

1987-1989 **Queens Public Library, Queens, NY.** Research Librarian. Supervised staff of five assistant research librarians. Responsible for research material acquisitions including four new computers for public use. Initiated co-operative program with area schools to introduce students to library resources.

1982-1987 **Amherst Public Library, Amherst, MA.** Assistant Librarian. Promoted to head librarian, 1985. Managed all aspects of daily operation of 100,000 volume collection. Facilitated library Senior Outreach Program and implemented children's Storytime Program.

1981-1982 **University of Massachusetts, Boston, MA.** Library Aide. Assisted staff with routine shelving duties, student and faculty reference requests, automated cataloguing of reserve materials. Awarded Outstanding Student Aide Award.

Education

1982   University of Massachusetts, MLS

1980   Brandeis University, BA

References
Available Upon Request

Nicole M. Franklin
8 Gaul Road North
Setauket, NY 11733
Home:(516) 555-9042
Work:(516) 555-1640

Work Experience

July 1993-present
> Setaucket Board of Education, East Setaucket,NY. Adult
> Education Family Literacy Educator. Instructor for
> pilot program that combines GED tutoring with
> family and parenting skills training. Member of
> teaching committee which designed program, developed
> instructional materials, and submitted proposal for
> state funding. Confer with Department of Social
> Services case workers to ensure program
> participants receive full range of services. Currently
> serving as a consultant to two area adult education
> programs.

August 1992-June 1993
> Setauket Board of Education, East Setauket, NY.
> Instructional Assistant/Clerk for the Even Start Family
> Literacy Program. Tutored individuals, performed
> administrative tasks, initiated fundraising to provide
> computers for classroom instruction. Collected and
> computerized Even Start data for statistical reporting
> to State Board of Education.

December 1989-July 1992
> Literacy Volunteer, Stoors, CT. Tutored adults in
> reading skills. Served on Volunteer Recruitment
> Committee. Trained new volunteers.

Education

1992   BA Psychology, University of Connecticut

References furnished on request

Salvador Mendez
6413 North Sheridan Road, #2B
Chicago, Illinois 60626
(312) 555-8623

Education:

10/93 - Present	Doctoral Student Institute for Clinical Social Work Chicago, Illinois
9/89 - 5/91	Boston University Boston, Massachusetts Master of Social Work
9/86 - 5/89	Bennet College Millbrook, New York Bachelor of Fine Arts

Experience:

7/91 - Present   **Social Worker**
Crisis Intervention and Referral Service
Lutheran General Hospital
Department of Psychiatry

Provide short-term and long-term
psychotherapy to individuals, couples,
and families. Conduct evaluations and
disposition planning for psychiatric
and emotionally traumatized patients
and their families in the Emergency
Room and Medical Clinic. Staff a
24-hour telephone hotline for suicide
prevention, crisis counseling, and/or
referrals. Community outreach and
training program involvement.

9/90 - 5/91   **Social Work Intern**
Massachusetts General Hospital
Boston, Massachusetts

Assigned to an affective disorder
inpatient unit. Provided family and
individual psychotherapy. Liaison
between the family and the hospital.
Responsible for family assessment,
discharge planning, and team treatment.

Salvador Mendez-page 1 of 2

7/90 - 4/91	**Counselor** Alternative Housing Systems Belmont, Massachusetts Provided counseling, crisis intervention, and supervision of house management tasks in a halfway house for ten adults with Borderline Personality Disorder.
9/89 - 5/90	**Social Work Intern** Cunningham House Mental Health Center Boston, Massachusetts Provided psychotherapy to individuals and groups, adults and children, with problems ranging from personality disorders, behavioral disturbances, anxiety, depression, and substance/ alcohol abuse. Cunningham House is a mental health clinic within a multiservice community agency.
10/88 - 8/89	**Literacy Volunteer** Millbrook Public Library Millbrook, New York Taught multilevel reading classes to primarily Hispanic and Eastern European immigrants in both classroom and industrial settings.

References Available Upon Request

Salvador Mendez-page 2 of 2

MARIE LOUISE BATELLE
670 West Church Street
Seattle, Washington 10602
(313) 555-3945

OBJECTIVE: Employment Counseling Position

PROFILE:

~Six years experience in public sector employment counseling
~Proven ability to prepare clients for the work force
~Excellent communications and organizational skills
~Effective liaison between federal agencies and local business
 community
~Innovative solutions to training and organizational challenges
~Diplomatic team player with strong leadership ability

EDUCATION:

B.A. Psychology   M Ed. Counseling
Western Washington University   University of California,
                                    Los Angeles

            Certified Personnel Counselor (CPC)
            National Association of Personnel Counselors

EXPERIENCE:

Women's Correctional Center
Seattle, Washington
Work Release Coordinator   1993-Present

Develop long-term occupational therapy program for female inmates
with focus on job skills, especially office skills and computer
literacy. Contact business owners to arrange entry-level
positions for inmates upon their release. Monitor
employment progress of released inmates. Found corporate
sponsor to donate computer equipment and software packages.

Washington Employment Opportunity Commission
Tacoma, Washington
Employment Counselor   1990-1993

Conducted job training class in basic clerical skills.
Administered occupational testing. Provided instruction
on resume preparation and employment interviewing skills.
Arranged job interviews for clients with participating area
businesses.

REFERENCES:

Will be furnished upon request

Greg Simon
947 W. Harwood Road
Lawrenceburg, IN 47025
(812) 555-5680

Work Experience

1993-Present	**Lawrenceburg Police Department** **Patrolman, Field Operations Division**
1992	**High School Liaison Officer** **Investigation Division** **Lawrenceburg High School** **Special Patrol** **Juvenile & Criminal Investigations**
1986-1992	**Indianapolis Police Department** **Staff Aide, Criminalistics Division**

Education

B.S. Law Enforcement Administration (Comprehensive Major Program combining Political Science, Sociology, and Psychology) from Indiana Central University, Indianapolis, IN, 1986

Police Training Institute, South Bend, IN, basic 10-week training, graduated #2 in class

Professional Certifications

Special Weapons & Tactics	Narcotics Investigation
Arson Investigation	Evidence Technician
Firearms Instructor	Breath Alcohol Testing

Professional Memberships

Fraternal Order of Police	Indiana Juvenile Officers

References Available Upon Request

Soo-Mi Chay
28 Elm Street
Brockton, MA 02403
(508) 555-6843

OBJECTIVE:

To empower clients to improve their lives through wise personal and career decisions.

EXPERIENCE:

Owner, Chay Associates, Inc. (1990-1995)

Achievements:

Provided successful private career counseling for a wide variety of corporate and individual clients

Developed and presented seminars for women returning to the work force

Conducted retirement-planning workshops for members of YMCA and local church organizations

Career consultant to Mount Holyoke College & assisted in organization and development of internship program at the college

Director, Mount Holyoke Career Center (1986-1990)

Achievements:

Provided career counseling and planning services to students

Organized and directed annual career fair

Conducted resume workshop for graduating seniors

Soo-Mi Chay-page 1 of 2

EDUCATION:

B.A., Psychology, University of New Mexico, 1983
M.A., Guidance and Counseling, California State
           University-Sacramento, 1985

PROFESSIONAL MEMBERSHIPS:

National Association of Counseling and Development
Career Education Association of New England
American Psychological Association

PUBLICATIONS:

"Job Search Strategies for Graduating Seniors,"
Career Bulletin, October, 1993

"Part-time Solutions for Working Mothers,"
Career Express, January, 1994

References Provided Upon Request

Soo-Mi Chay-page 2 of 2

Allan A. MacFarlan
5448 Fournier Road
Westerly, RI 02891
(401) 555-4191

Objective: To obtain a library science position that utilizes my skills in developing and maintaining a large collection of texts and assisting patrons or students with research projects.

Work Experience (1989-Present)

Head Librarian, Providence College, Providence, RI

Responsible for acquisition decisions for college library

Direct staff of 5 librarians

Develop annual budget recommendations

Previous Position (1978-1989)

Reference Librarian, Westerly Public Library

Responsible for cataloging and maintenance of reference collection

Organized and directed after-hours reference service

Education

M.A., Library Science, Rosary College, 1983
B.A., English, Northern Illinois University, 1978

References Available

Mary A. Griffin
102 N. Edgewater Court
Easton, PA 18042
(215) 555-8815

Professional Experience

Director
Easton Community Senior Center, Easton, PA, 1980-1995

Public Relations
Developed membership program through increase of services and incentives
Designed and developed a monthly newsletter using desktop publishing systems
Arranged press confrences and prepared press kits
Participated in community events and gave presentations at civic functions
Financial Management
Prepared annual reports and monthly statements
Developed a computerized bookkeeping system
Created a volunteer work force of over 40 members
Wrote grant proposals and implemented fund-raising activities to provide over 90% of the budget
Increased budget by 80% during tenure
Program Development
Created and implemented fifty activities including healthcare, educational, and legal services
Organized recreational programs, classes, trips, and special events
Awards
Governor's Hometown Award, 1994

Teacher
Shelton School 1975-1980

Taught third and fourth grade classes

Education

University of Pittsburgh: Certificate of Business Administration
                    Law Program for Community Developers

Point Park College: Bachelor of Science/Education

Skills

Macintosh computer systems; word processing, database, desktop publishing, spreadsheet
Budgeting and finance
Strong organizational, management, marketing, and sales skills

References Available on Request

JANET K. SCHAFER, L.C.S.W.
1026 River Road
Columbia, MO 65201
(314) 555-1678

PROFESSIONAL OBJECTIVE:
A position as a psychotherapist in a clinical setting using proven skills in assessment; treatment, planning, and delivery; individual, couple, family, and group treatment.

QUALIFICATIONS:
Master of Social Work Degree, University of Missouri, 1992. Four years experience in mental health in hospital psychiatric unit, community mental health center, drug dependence treatment center, and hospital outpatient unit. Experienced in program planning and delivery and working with the elderly. Excellent communications, negotiations, team-building and problem-solving skills.

EXPERIENCE:
1993-1995 <u>Crisis Therapist</u> Boone Hospital Center

Staff a 24-hour telephone hotline for suicide prevention, crisis counseling, and/or referral.

Provide brief intensive psychotherapy to individuals, couples, and families who need immediate treatment for a variety of emotional crises such as a death or divorce, and victims of accidents and assaults. Treat patients for symptoms such as anxiety, panic disorder, depression, post-traumatic stress disorder, and adjustment reactions to marital and family problems.

Conduct emergency-room evaluations of persons who present with symptoms of chronic mental illness or any kind of emotional trauma such as rape or domestic violence.

Janet K. Schafer-page 1 of 2

1990-1993 <u>Addiction Therapist</u> Holy Cross Hospital

Conducted assessments for alcohol and/or drug addiction. Provided therapy for individuals and couples recovering from alcohol and/or drug addiction or the effects of the addiction of other family members.

1989-1990 <u>Intern Therapist</u> Wetzel Center/U. of Missouri

Provided therapy to individuals, couples and families with variety of presenting problems including addiction, incest, narcissistic personality disorders.

Participated in intensive intervention program which serves families in crisis. Worked in innovative short-term family program which emphasizes immediate solutions.

Provided appropriate referrals to meet individual needs of clients and client systems.

1988-1991 <u>Intern Therapist</u> St. Luke Medical Center

Provided therapy for chronically mentally ill patients and their families. Served as support for patients in hospital.

Participated in interdisciplinary treatment program. Collaborated with nurses, social workers, psychiatrists.

EDUCATION:

1992	**Master of Social Work/University of Missouri**
1986	**Bachelor of Arts/Kenyon College**

References furnished upon request.

Janet K. Schafer-page 2

VELIO A. PANSERA
8415 Oketo Avenue
Niles, Illinois 60714
(708) 555-7102

CAREER OBJECTIVE: To obtain a position as a school
psychologist.

EDUCATION: National-Louis University Evanston, IL
Degree: Educational Specialist in School
Psychology, 1995

Loyola University Chicago, IL
Degree: Master of Arts
Clinical Psychology, 1993

Illinois State University Normal, IL
Degree: Bachelor of Arts, 1990
Sociology/Psychology

CERTIFICATION: Type 73 Illinois School Board of Education

WORK EXPERIENCE:

8/94-1995 Glenview North High School   Glenview, IL
School Psychology Intern

-Administer and interpret psychological
 and educational diagnostic tests
-Lead group counselling sessions
-Conduct individual counselling sessions
-Teach social skills classes to special
 education students

-Coach Junior Girls' Softball

8/93-8/94 Martin Academy   Niles, IL
Therapist and Teacher Assistant

-Worked as a team member to develop
 appropriate levels of academic and
 behavioral assistance for students
 ages 10 to 19
-Participated in crisis intervention team
-Directed group therapy sessions

Velio A. Pansera-page 1 of 2

1/93-6/93 <u>Tauber Mental Health Center</u>   Mundelein, IL
Psychology Intern

-Administered psychological tests
-Counselled chemically dependent adolescents
-Conducted individual and group therapy

Summer 92 <u>Niles Park District</u> Niles, IL
Volleyball Day Camp Supervisor

-Taught basic fundamentals of volleyball to
 boys and girls ages 9 to 17
-Explained team strategies and instructed
 students on how to execute strategies

Fall 1990 <u>St. Lukes Academy</u> Des Plaines, IL
Internship-Family Educator

-Served as a family educator for a home
 housing young women ages 6 to 17
-Worked with physically, emotionally,
 mentally, and sexually abused young women
-Assisted in the application of a behavior
 modification system

Fall 1989 <u>Illinois State University</u>   Normal, IL
Student Volunteer-Head Start Program

-Assisted in classroom activities
-Worked with children ages 3 to 5

MEMBERSHIPS: American Psychological Association
               Illinois School Psychologists Association

References Available

Velio A. Pansera-page 2 of 2

CHRISTINA RIVERA

607 Ramsey Drive
Arlington, Virginia 22209
(703) 555-2821

CAREER OBJECTIVE:

Seeking a full-time teaching position in an urban public school that enables me to combine my primary level teaching experience with my newly acquired Special Education degree.

EDUCATION:

Indiana University, Bloomington, Indiana: B.S., Elementary Education;
    May 1992
University of Virginia, Charlottesville: M. Ed.,
    Learning Disabilities/Behavior Disorders, December 1994

CERTIFICATION:

Virginia Standard Teaching License, Grades K-9, June 1992
Virginia Special Education, Learning Disabilities and
    Social/Emotional Disorders, December 1994

PROFESSIONAL EXPERIENCE:

Kindergarten teacher, St. Margaret Mary School, Arlington, VA, 1993-1995
Kindergarten teacher, St. Francis School, Richmond, VA, 1992-1993
Student teacher, St. Francis School, Grade 4, January-May, 1992

RELATED EXPERIENCE:

Special Education Tutor, Learning Center, Richmond, Virginia, 1994
Camp Counselor, Camp Deerpath, Baltimore, Maryland, 1992
Volunteer, Junior High Girls' Club leader, Richmond Community Center,
    summers 1988-1991

Christina Rivera-page 1 of 2

ACTIVITIES AND HONORS:

Curriculum Committee, St. Margaret Mary School, 1994
Science Fair Committee, St. Francis School, 1993
Talent Show Committee, St. Francis School, 1993
Chair, Philanthropy Committee, Delta Delta Delta Sorority
Chair, Alumna Relations, Delta Delta Delta Sorority
Outstanding College Senior Award, Delta Delta Delta Sorority

PROFESSIONAL MEMBERSHIPS:

Orton Dyslexia Society
Indiana University School of Education Professional Organization,
Program Committee
Indiana University Student Foundation, Special Projects Committee

REFERENCES:

Mary Price, Principal, St. Margaret Mary School, Arlington, Virginia
John Cook, Vice-Principal, St. Margaret Mary School, Arlington, Virginia
Barb Fenwick, Supervisor, Learning Center, Richmond, Virginia
Michael Hernandez, Former Principal, St. Francis School, Richmond, Virginia

Christina Rivera-page 2 of 2

THOMAS LUTHRA
33 Humphreys Street
Washington, DC 20059
Home: (301) 555-8913
Business: (301) 555-5347
Fax: (301) 555-5624

BACKGROUND

Expertise in individual and group guidance and counseling of faculty, students, and administrators in career, personal, and academic concerns; international business experience; efficient and effective management skills; diverse public speaking, consulting, and instructional experience in America and abroad.

ADMINISTRATION/COORDINATION

Director, Career Planning Center, Howard University, Washington, DC, 1982-Present

* Administer career development program for liberal arts students, faculty, staff, representatives of employing institutions, and representatives of graduate and professional schools

* Supervise staff of nineteen: four assistant directors, three secretaries, and twelve students.

* Plan, implement, and coordinate seminars, workshops, counseling and referral services, and dissemination of career information to appropriate constituencies.

* Provide special counseling and advice for prelaw and science students interested in business, public service, and international affairs.

Associate Dean of Students, Howard University, 1989-Present

* <u>Ex-officio member</u>, Graduate Fellowship Committee, Howard University, 1981-1995.
  Advise and counsel students applying for such fellowships, scholarships, and grants as Mellon, Fulbright, Rhodes, Marshall, Watson, Churchill, and St. Andrews; campus liaison with above sponsors; prepare credentials of applicants for review by committee.

Chair, Search Committee for College President, Howard University, 1990

Chair, Search Committee for Dean of Students, Howard University, 1989

Thomas Luthra-page 1 of 3

ADMINISTRATION/COORDINATION (Continued)

Assistant Dean for Supportive Services, Howard University, 1987-1989

* Supervised professional staff of seven including Assistant Director of University Scholars Program, Director of Math Clinic, Director of Writing Program, and Director of the Higher Educational Opportunity Program, with Washington, DC Department of Education.

* Managed budget of $840,000.

Chair, Search Committee for Director of Writing Program, 1988

Associate Dean of Students, Missouri Southern State College, Joplin, MO, 1988

Counseled and guided students regarding personal, educational, and career concerns. Served on tripartite committees such as Judicial Board, Curriculum Committee, and Campus Council.

Director, Career Planning, Missouri Southern State College, 1976-1982

* Administered career development program for liberal arts students, faculty, administrators, and representatives of prospective employers
* Designed workshops and seminars, including Life Planning, Decision Making, New Directions (career exploration).

Director/Consultant, Tehran English Language Institute, Tehran, Iran, 1974-1976

Administered teaching programs in conjunction with Iranian Ministries of Education and Higher Education.

CONSULTATION

Consultant/Counselor, Thomas J. Watson Foundation, Northeastern University, Boston, MA, summer 1990

Counseled sixty returning Watson Fellows regarding fellowship year.

Head, Evaluation Team, Career Development Office, Stanford University, Stanford, CA, 1986

Thomas Luthra-page 2 of 3

EDUCATION

Invited Participant, International Seminar on Career Planning
Oxford University, Oxford, England, fall 1994

Participant, Institute for Educational Guidance, Stanford
University, Stanford, CA, summer 1989

M.A., Teaching English as a Foreign Language, Teachers College,
Columbia University, New York, NY, 1974

M.Ed., Religious Education and Counseling, University of Southern
Maine, Portland, ME, 1968

Course Work, Middle Eastern Culture, History, and Religion,
University of Tehran, Tehran, Iran, 1968-1969

B.B.A., Economics and Business Administration, Westminister College,
New Wilmington, PA, 1962

PUBLICATIONS

Life's Work, Chicago, IL: The Career Press, 1995.

"The ESL Conversation Class," English Teaching Journal, vol. V
(March-April, 1991), no. 1, 19-20. Republished in English
Teaching Journal, Special Issue, vol. XIV, 1993.

"Career Counseling and the Minority Student," in New Directions in
the 1990s: Career Development, edited by Christopher Wendt.
New York: Academic Press, 1990.

AWARDS

Silver Medal Award for alumni service to Howard University. Council
for Advancement and Support of Education, 1991.

Recipient, Faculty Development Award, Howard University, 1989

MEMBERSHIPS

College Personnel Officers

National Association of Prelaw Advisors

References Available Upon Request

Thomas Luthra-page 3 of 3

Sandra Swierczynski
200 E. Third Avenue
Lowell, MA 01854
(508) 555-4732

1993   Director, Campus Counseling Center, Lowell University, Lowell Mass.
to
Present   Direct university counseling service providing educational,
          vocational, and personal counseling to Lowell students, faculty, and
          staff. Supervise staff of three: counselor, administrative assistant, and
          student intern. Conduct extensive outreach program in campus community.
          Present workshops on topics such as stress management and
          assertiveness.

1989   Owner, Private Counseling Practice, Brockton, Mass.
to
1992   Provided personal, educational, and career counseling to individuals,
          groups, and corporations. Assisted private corporations with outplacement
          programs. Consultant to Brockton Community Health Center, helped design
          and implement crisis intervention hotline.

1985   Counselor, Brockton Public School System, Brockton, Mass.
to
1989   Administered and interpreted vocational interest inventories.
          Provided career information and counseling to public school students.

<u>Education</u>

| University of Virginia | 1985 | M.Ed. | Counseling |
| Knox College | 1983 | B.A. | English |

<u>Professional Memberships</u>

New England Vocational Guidance Association
American Society for Vocational Counseling

REFERENCES AVAILABLE

Bok Chul Lee
475 Park Drive
Chicago, IL 60613
312-555-8645

Objective:

To pursue a career in criminal or social service setting working for, and with, minors.

Education:

M.A.	Northwestern University The School of Social Work Concentration: Clinical Social Work	Evanston, IL June, 1995
B.A.	Northeastern Illinois University Major: Criminal Justice Minor: Social Work High Honors List	Chicago, IL December, 1992
A.A.	Malcom-X College Major: Liberal Studies	Chicago, IL December, 1990

Professional Experience:

Cook County Services, Caseworker III   *Chicago, IL*
November 1994-Present

Conduct investigations and submit intensive social studies involving private adoption placements and contested adoptions. In addition, responsibilities include investigating, by court order, the social conditions and residences of children whose parents are involved in divorce, paternity, and probate-related custody and visitation issues. Serve as an expert witness when subpoenaed.

Bok Chul Lee-page 1 of 2

Professional Internships:

Board of Education, Chicago Public School System   Chicago, IL
September 1993-June 1994

Provided individual, family, and group treatment to children and their families. Participated in child placements with a multi-discipline staff.

Office of the Public Guardian   Chicago, IL
January 1993- September 1993

Interviewed children and adolescents to assess and document factual background of abuse and/or neglect prior to court hearings. Assessment concluded with in-home evaluation.

Circuit Court of Cook County/Juvenile Division   Chicago, IL
Spring 1992

Assisted probation officers with court duties on cases related to minor respondents, participated in field surveillance and home visits of minors, and completed and filed monthly and quarterly reports of minors' progess.

Professional Memberships:

Illinois Social Work Council
National Association of Social Workers

References:

Available on request

Bok Chul Lee-page 2 of 2

David Swanson
**650 Clifton Avenue
Austin, TX 68143
(612) 555-6915**

Skills:

Supervision

-Directed Head Start training program, evaluated teaching performances
-Recruited and trained Outward Bound volunteers
-Supervised work/study program, monitored students' job performance
 and employer satisfaction, recruited corporate participants

Program Design & Organization

-Established course objectives, developed curriculum for Head Start
-Designed training program for Outward Bound Volunteers
-Coordinated adult education program with government, corporate, and
 community agencies

Communications

-Wrote federal grant proposal and lobbied for funding for Head Start
-Presented lectures to community and professional groups
-Developed training guides for Outward Bound volunteers

Teaching

-Developed instructional aids and educational materials for adolescents
 and adults
-Increased motivation and program completion rates among at-risk
 students in adult education program

David Swanson-page 1 of 2

Employment:

1990-Present   Director, Adult Education Program
High School District 84
Austin, TX

1987-1990   Director
Head Start
Atlanta, GA

1986-1987   Program Coordinator
Outward Bound
Atlanta, GA

Education:

Georgia State University M.Ed.   Adult Education, 1990

Southern Methodist University B.A.   English, 1986

Honors:

Outstanding Teacher Award, 1990

Atlanta Community Service Medal, 1989

Memberships:

American Society of Training and Development

References:

Available on Request

THERESA PORTER
2453 CAMBRIDGE ROAD
KANSAS CITY, MO 64108

JOB OBJECTIVE: A library science position that will utilize my management and materials acquisitions skills

CAPABILITIES:

*Review purchasing materials and suggest acquisitions
*Develop budgets
*Act as community liaison
*Create publicity materials
*Study and report on the condition of special collections
*Handle reference calls and requests

ACHIEVEMENTS:

*Developed community outreach program that increased library use
*Developed successful budget proposals
*Trained volunteers
*Supervised staff of six
*Updated and expanded reference library
*Developed specialized science collection

EMPLOYMENT HISTORY:

1991-Present	Librarian	Kansas City Public Libraries
1986-Present	Head Librarian	Wright High School

EDUCATION:

Rosary College	1986	MLS	Library Science
New York University	1984	BS	Biology

REFERENCES AVAILABLE

Milton R. Rosenburg
650 Second Street
Portland, OR 97204
(503) 555-6418

EXPERIENCE

Counselor, Portland Mental Health Center, Portland, OR, 1993-Present

Counsel youth and adult population, suggest treatment options for drug and alcohol dependence. Refer patients to other private and community organizations for medical and social support. Maintain accurate, detailed records of weekly counseling sessions. Organize and lead ongoing addiction support groups.

Coordinator, Seattle Community Recreation Center, Seattle, WA, 1990-93

Planned and created this community recreation center to provide supervised activities for local youth. Wrote funding proposal for town council. Recruited volunteer staff and members. Purchased all supplies. Designed publicity materials.

Student Activities Director, Pacific Lutheran U., Tacoma, WA, 1986-90

Planned and directed student activities including live entertainment and special events. Supervised student activities committee. Booked and publicized events. Supervised staff of four.

EDUCATION

University of Oregon   1985   BS   Leisure & Recreation

SKILLS

Word-processing and Desktop publishing ability
Fluent in Spanish and French

PROFESSIONAL ASSOCIATIONS

Portland Youth Council
National Recreation Alliance

REFERENCES AVAILABLE ON REQUEST

ANN OLIVERA
664 E. Ivy Drive
Nashville, TN 37212

Experience

1991-Present   Supervisor, Intake Unit,
                              Greater Nashville Social Services

Duties include the supervision of four workers assigned to interview
and assess parties involved in private adoption proceedings.
Log, track, and assign cases. Witness consents by biological
parents for the adoption of their children. Record fees for adoption
studies and subpoenas. Review and plan strategies (with collaboration
of coworkers) on "problem" cases.

1985-1991 Caseworker/Child Custody Worker
                     Greater Nashville Social Services

Handled approximately 1,000 child custody mediation cases and
over 50 child custody and adoption investigations. Experience in
Municipal Division (in parentage cases) and in Domestic Relations
Division. Mediator and expert witness. Handled emergency cases.

1983-1985 Part-time Counselor/Office Manager, Office of Veterans
                     Affairs, Tenessee State University

Advised student veterans on many issues and supervised other
employees in these capacities. Helped to write and edit proposal for
program funding; helped to determine and allocate budget.

Education

1990 Master's Degree in Social Work, Hillcrest School of Social Work

Concentration in mental health. Clinical internship at Nashville Family
Services, Child and Adolescent Unit, 1990-1991. Acted as therapist,
making provisional diagnoses, and consulting with staff.
Clinical internship at Providence Crisis Center 1989-1990. Provided
services to victims and perpetrators of domestic violence.
Served as therapist and intake evaluator.

                              Ann Olivera-page 1 of 2

Education (cont.)

1983 Master of Arts in Teaching (with honors), Temple Univeristy

Thesis/Research Project: "Analysis of Gender Differences in the Syntax of Student Writing."

1980 Bachelor of Arts, Magna Cum Laude, City College of New York

Publications

Article, "Decision-Making Alternatives in Child Custody Mediation," in Family Counseling Quarterly, vol. 7, no. 3, spring 1993.

Work in progress: "Security Issues at Women's Shelters: Implications for Domestic Violence Treatment."

References

Lynne Schickel, Former Supervisor, Providence Crisis Center, now a marriage and family counseling mediator in private practice: (615) 555-8965.

John Gilroy, Director, Nashville Family Services and Community Mental Health Center: (615) 555-8756.

James Kortis, Supervisor, Greater Nashville Social Services: (615) 555-4321.

Professional Memberships and Licensures

State of Tennessee Licensed Social Worker
Member, National Association of Social Workers
Member, American Alliance for the Prevention of Domestic Violence

Ann Olivera-page 2 of 2

Resume of Education and Employment

Susan Parsons
614 North White Street
Arlington Heights, IL 60004
(708) 555-8604

Education

B.S./R.N.   Northern Illinois University, DeKalb, Illinois

Type 73 special service certificate

Employment

January 1991 to Present	Instructor of Family Living at Glenwood High School, Young Adult Education Program
October 1986 to January 1991	Parental Leave
August 1984 to October 1986	School Nurse, Wheaton Elementary School, District 63. Responsible for participation in child study team, development of health curriculum, vision and hearing screenings, and first aid.
July1981 to August 1984	Public Health Nurse, DuPage County Health Department, Wheaton, Illinois. Responsible for school nursing, organization of, and participation in, well-child clinic, home care of elderly and ill, supervision of home health aides,and cooperative programs with the mental health department.

References Available on Request

Thomas Brooks
81 Hill Street
San Francisco, CA 94165

OBJECTIVE: A position in health policy administration that makes use of my expertise as a disease control specialist.

SKILLS:
      *Ability to conduct investigations, develop & implement disease control
      *Knowledge of public health administration
      *Health care crisis management skills
      *Disciplined work habits, strong organizational skills
      *Ability to meet tight deadlines & function smoothly under pressure

EXPERIENCE:

      *Extensive background in public health
      *Experience in San Francison Department of Health with Dr. Stevens
      *Investigated outbreak of Asian Flu in San Francisco public schools
      *Published paper on blood shortage in National Journal of Health
      *Claims adjustor for United Insurance Company

EMPLOYMENT:

Medical Technologist, San Francisco Community Blood Bank
1989-Present

Disease Control Consultant, San Francisco Department of Health
1985-1989

Claims Adjustor, United Insurance Company
1982-1985

EDUCATION:

M.A. in Public Health, University of California at Davis

REFERENCES AVAILABLE UPON REQUEST

Martha Clarke
944 Grace Street
Modesto, CA   93201
916-555-5642

Professional Background

Diverse professional with experience in the following: compilation and statistical analysis of medical and scientific data, abstracting and indexing of technical material, medical library science, clinical laboratory work.

Skills

Leadership ability, strong management skills, public speaking experience, excellent organizational skills

Employment History

Hughes Pharmaceutical Supply
86 White Street
Modesto, CA
1992-Present
Position: Medical Reference Librarian

Abstract and index articles from medical reference material; compile research materials for sales, legal, and marketing professionals.

Warren County Hospital
162 Lincoln Drive
Sacramento, CA
1990-1992
Position: Medical Records Supervisor

Created on-line medical records system. Supervised medical records clerks. Created standardized records procedure and conducted in-service seminars on use of new system for all affected departments.

Martha Clarke-page 1 of 2

Davis General Hospital
1844 West Street
Davis, California
1987-1990
Position: Clinical Laboratory Technician

Performed clinical testing of medical specimens. Collected data for statistical analysis of all tests.

Education

Coursework in Library Science, University of San Francisco
Medical Laboratory Technology Program, Parkins Community College, Davis
License: American Medical Technology Association
B.S. in Biology, University of California, Davis

References will be provided upon request

Martha Clarke-page 2 of 2

Catherine Walker
664 Prospect Avenue
Dover, Delaware 19901
(606) 555-5346

Objective: To obtain a position as a special education assistant in
a school or residential setting.

Skills: Team teaching
Tutoring
Nursing assistance
Understanding of emotional, behavioral & learning disabilities
Fluent in Spanish

Education: 1993, B.A. in Sociology, Delaware State College
Coursework in Special Education at Delaware State, part-time,
working toward an M.A. in Special education

Member of New England chapter of Association for Children and Adults
with Learning Disabilities

**Work
History:** Staff Assistant , 1994-Present, Gateway Services

Aid professional staff of this residential program for handicapped adults.
Assist in providing educational services, occupational therapy,
and nursing services.

Teacher's Assistant, 1993-1994, Elementary School District 58

Classroom experience with students affected by emotional & behavioral
difficulties, and learning disabilities. Assisted in preparation and
implementation of individualized lesson plans for students. Provided
progress reports to teacher, parents, and school psychologist.

References Available on Request

Juanita Lopez
16 Cutriss Street
St. Louis, MO 63105
(314) 555-8967

*Compassionate nursing   **Dedicated Teamwork*   **Supportive Family Counseling*

BACKGROUND

Experienced staff nurse with specialized education and training in serving the health care needs of elderly clients. Currently seeking employment in a geriatric residential or day care facility. Previous employment in hospital, clinic, and home health situations. Teaching experience.

EMPLOYMENT HISTORY

Visiting Nurse, Elder Support Services of St. Louis, 1992-Present
Staff Nurse, Kingston Clinic, St. Louis, 1990-1992
Instructor, Adams College BSN Program, Elmhurst, IL, 1986-1990
Staff Nurse, Bethany General Hospital, Oak Park, IL, 1980-1986

EDUCATION AND LICENSURE

BSN, Northern Illinois University
Registered Nurse, licensed in the states of Illinois and Missouri

ACHIEVEMENTS

*Supervise staff of 12 LPNs and nursing assistants for home health care agency
*Provide emotional support for patient families & referral to appropriate agencies
*Managed large, diverse caseload at urban helath clinic
*Participated in ongoing curriculum design & evaluation for BSN program
*Developed and facilitated educational in-service programs for hospital medical staff

References Available

Tyrell Davis
1811 Green Street
Cleveland, Ohio 44122
(216) 555-7837--Work
(216) 555-3659--Home

OBJECTIVE

Position in criminal corrections with potential to lead to supervisory/
administrative work.

EDUCATION

Ohio State University, B.A. Degree, 1991
Major: Criminal Justice
Minors: Social Service & Political Science
Freshman Dorm Manager during my senior year

EMPLOYMENT

Cleveland Youth Authority, Corrections Department, Parole Division
Position: Parole Officer (1991-Present)
Supervisor: Walter Reed
Duties:*Supervise parole procedures for Cleveland Boys School and
Ohio Youth Correctional Center; prepare home evaluations,
social histories, and interviews with inmates. *Assess
inmates' social problems; supervise juvenile offenders; counsel
inmates and their families. *Arrange residence, education, and
employment for prospective parolees. *Represent Cleveland
Youth Authority at community functions and hearings; act as
community liaison. *Prosecute parole violators.

Reference available from current supervisor, Walter Reed,
(216) 555-7839.
Detailed references upon request.

Roger Boyd
673 Drake Street
Pittsburgh, PA 15234
Phone: 412-555-6453

Job Objective:

A legal position with a social service agency

Employment:

1993-Present

District Attorney's Office, Pittsburgh
Assistant District Attorney
Criminal Courts Division

Take depositions from witnesses and complaintants.
Prepare cases for trial: legal research and writing,
filing of motions.

1990-1993

Morgan & Ryan Legal Corporation, Pittsburgh
Law Clerk

Interviewed clients for attorneys.
Filed court documents.
Standardized manual office procedures and fully
computerized office.

1988-1990

Warren County Department of Social Services
Warren, PA
Caseworker II

Established family eligibility for food stamps, public aid,
medicare, and other programs. Maintained average
caseload of 75-125 clients at a time.

Education:

B.A. in Sociology, University of Pittsburgh
J.D. Northwestern University, Chicago, IL

References Available Upon Request

Margaret Chang

1483 Kathleen Court, Westport, CT 06880, Phone: 203-555-4523

Psychiatric Social Worker

Summary

Trained psychiatric social worker comfortable in a variety of settings, experienced in dealing with diverse client population, seeking new opportunities to assist clients with social and psychiatric adjustment needs.

Work History

Home Health Caseworker, Lutheran Social Services of New England, 1989 to Present

Provide comprehensive discharge planning for patients leaving Lutheran Community Hospital. Referral to appropriate community services and programs for nursing, child care, housekeeping, counseling, and other ongoing needs.

Intake Counselor, Wheeler Psychiatric Institute, 1985-1989

Conducted initial interviews with patients and family memebers. Explained the Institute's programs and fees, patient's rights and responsibilities. Assisted patients and family members with decision to admit. Referred patients to appropriate community services.

Counselor, Westport Women's Center, 1983-1985

Provided private counseling for area women related to personal and career goals. Developed support groups for women dealing with issues of substance abuse and incest survival.

Margaret Chang-page 1 of 2

Education

M.S.W.	*Columbia School of Social Work*
B.A.	*Boston College/Major:Psychology*

Skills

Computer literate
Fluent in Spanish & French
Knowledge of Sign Language

References

Available upon request

Margaret Chang-page 2 of 2

Roberta Morise

Address: 67 Gray Street
Marietta, Georgia 30067

Phone: 404-555-5849 (home)
404-5554738 (office)

Community /Recreation Services Professional

*Vocational & Personal Counseling
*Youth Recreational Services
*Community-based Social Services

Qualifications

Extensive paid and volunteer experience with range of
community organizations. Previous positions in public sector
and private, not-for-profit groups. Demonstrated
excellence in program design and implementation,
counseling, fundraising, supervision of volunteers.

Key Skills

*Publicity	*Supervision
*Desktop Publishing	*Office Management
*Basic Bookkeeping	*Counseling

Employment

Director, Jr. Achievement of Georgia (1991-Present)

Establish and manage Jr. Achievement programs in Georgia schools.
Coordinate publicity efforts. Recruit volunteer project directors.
Solicit funds from local business leaders. Compile statistics
and project summaries for national office.

Roberta Morise-page 1 of 2

Day Care Coordinator, Grove Street YMCA, Marietta (1987-1991)

Supervised preschool and summer camp programs. Assisted in hiring of instructors and camp counselors. Trained counselors. Supervised production of publicity materials. Coordinated registration.

Guidance/Vocationl Counselor, Marietta Public High School (1984-1987)

Counseled students regarding personal and educational issues. Assisted with course scheduling and college entrance planning. Administered vocational testing. Assisted director of work/study program.

Volunteer Work

Board Member: Marietta Women's Club
Maretta Public Library

Volunteer: St. Theresa's Homeless Shelter

Education

M.S. Counseling University of Virginia
B.S. History Mississippi State University

Roberta Morise-page 2 of 2

Gary King 33 Elm Street Jackson, MS 39216 601-555-9076

Counseling Experience

Jackson Memorial Hospital, Jackson, MS
Crisis Counselor, 3/90-Present

Provide crisis intervention and emergency counseling for patients and families. Assist hospital personnel and local authorities with suspected child abuse cases. Refer patients to social service agencies for grief counseling, hospice care, substance abuse treatment, and other services. Design individual discharge plans for psychiatric patients.

Glendale Nursing Pavillion, Jackson, MS
Counseling Specialist, 8-86 - 3/90

Administered psychiatric evaluations to new patients. Organized and conducted support groups for residents' family members. Provided counseling forresidents. Arranged educational seminars for staff.

Education

B.S.	Human Services	Columbia University, New York
M.S.W.	In Progress	Mississippi State University
Courses		Hospital Law Enforcement Policies
		AIDS Awareness
		Elder Abuse
		Theories of Group Therapy
		Women & Substance Abuse

*Familiar with Lotus1-2-3 and other softwre programs
*C.P.R. Certification
*Conversant in Spanish and Italian

References

Mary Romano, Director, In-patient Mental Health, Jackson Memorial, 601-555-7969
Gary Oldes, Director, Glendale Nursing Pavillion, 601-555-8903

Gloria Price
17 Dayton Street
Tempe, Arizona 85281
602-555-8057

Overview

Secondary school principal and former teacher with 12 years of experience. Extensive background in budgets, community relations, teacher contract negotiations

Capabilities

Administration of large public and private high schools. Principal of 1500-student suburban public high schoool, former principal of 1200-student private academy.

Supervision of teachers and school staff. Supervised 80 unionized public high school teachers. Directed staff of 65 teachers and other personnel at private academy.

Preparation and management of $1-$6 million school budgets.

Successful fundraising drives and grant proposals to fund new construction and repair of existing facilities.

Curriculum design for new computer literacy program for high school district.

District representative for teacher contract negotiations.

Four years' experience as high school English instructor.

Experience

8/89 to Present   *Principal, Maine County Hight School, Tempe, AZ*

1/84 to 5/89   *Principal, St. Vincent's Academy, Yuma, AZ*

9/80 to 1/84   *English Instructor, Alamar High School, Houston, TX*

Gloria Price-page 1 of 2

Education

B.A. English
Southern Methodist University
Dallas, Texas

M.S. Public School Administration
Arizona State University
Tempe, Arizona

Publications

"Computer Literacy and Facilities Design," Curriculum Review, vol. 81, March 1994

"The Multicultural Classroom," Instructor, vol.21, number 2, January 1995

Personal

Desire to relocate to Chicago area. Willing to travel to Chicago for personal interview. Available Fall 1995.

References

Excellent professional references available upon request.

Gloria Price-page 2 of 2

Frank Madden
8053 Windsor Drive
Cincinnati, OH 45242
(513) 555-4380

OWNER   Madden Translation & Interpretation Services

Established 1989. Professional translation and
interpretation service for health care, legal,
and other professionals. Staff of six. Languages
include German, Spanish, French, Russian, Korean.

PARTIAL CLIENT LIST

*Cincinnati General Hospital

Translate documents and act as interpreter for
health care staff.

*Kepler & Associates, Ltd.

Assist attorneys in taking depositions, translate
documents, interpret during courtroom proceedings.

*Catholic Charities, Adoption Services Division

Translation of documents and interpretation services
pertaining to international adoptions.

EDUCATION

B.A. Modern Languages   University of California
                          Berkeley, California

SKILLS

Extensive international travel
Knowledge of WordPerfect and Lotus 1-2-3

COMMUNITY SERVICE

Advisor to International Students at Xavier College
ESL Tutor, Cincinnati Public Library

REFERENCES AVAILABLE ON REQUEST

Holly Smith
14 Randall Road
Atlanta, GA 30315

Job Objective

Camp counselor position for the summer of 1995

Education

University of Alabama, B.S. degree in progress
Expected graduation date: June, 1996
Major: Psychology/Child Development
Minor: Recreation & Leisure

Certifications

Red Cross trained & certified swimming instructor
C.P.R. certified

Employment

Summer 1994   Counselor, Jr. Adventure Camp, Atlanta

Supervised, with 3 other counselors, a group of 50 children, ages 7 to 10, at park district day camp. Led games, explained craft projects, supervised field trips and weekly visits to the local water park.

1993-1994   Day Care Worker, Kids' Place, Tuscaloosa

Worked 15 hours per week during sophomore year at local day care center. Responsible for playground supervision, recreational activities, and routine care of children aged 6 months to 5 years.

Summer 1993   Swimming Instructor, Water World, Atlanta

Swimming instructor in Red Cross approved swimming program for ages 4 to 10. Planned and conducted swimming lessons ,evaluated students for proper class assignment, acted as lifeguard.

References Furnished Upon Request

Renu Patel
45 Washington Street
Rochester, New York 14611
Phone 716-555-8945

Employment

1987-Present (Currently on Leave)	Assistant Professor of English University of Richmond Richmond, Virginia

Specialist in Victorian literature. Conduct literature and writing classes. Faculty advisor. Extensive committee work. Published scholar.

1986-1987	Composition Instructor University of Iowa Iowa City, Iowa

Taught first-year composition students. Conducted composition courses, administered writing competency exams to first-year students, tutored at writing lab.

Education

Ph.D.	English	University of Chicago
B.A.	English	Kenyon College

Publications (Partial List)

"The Forgotten Bronte: Anne Bronte and the Gondal Saga,"
Victorian Studies Quarterly, vol. xxii, April 1994.

"Literary Merit and the Multicultural Syllabus," Journal of College English,
 Spring 1993.

Editor, Shakespeare's Sisters: Essays on Women Writers. New York:
University Press, 1992.

DETAILED C.V. & REFERENCES AVAILABLE

John Parker
Nutritionist

17 Oak Lane* Omaha, NE 61855 * 402-555-6579

WORK HISTORY: Chief Dietician
St. Vincent's Hospital
483 Prentiss Circle
Omaha, Nebraska
Dates: 6/83 to Present

Duties include budget development and approval. Menu
planning and supervision of patient food preparation.
Supervision of food procurement. Interaction with medical
staff to develop individualized diets that assist patients'
recovery. Assure compliance with health & safety codes.

Dietitian
Terrence Community College
653 Rogers Parkway
Omaha, Nebraska
Dates: 7/80 to 6/83

Menu planning and supervision of food preparation for food
services department. Duties included daily meals and catering
for special on-campus events. Participated in plans for
 redesign and expansion of student cafeteria.

EDUCATION: B.S.   Nutrition   Northern Illinois University
Honors: Dean's List last three years

REFERENCES: Available on Request

Ernestine Jones
64 West 62nd Street, #3B
Brooklyn, New York 11210
Home Phone: 212-555-8935

Abilities

~ Thorough knowledge of eligibility requirements for New York State public welfare programs
~ Experience handling large, complex caseloads
~ Knowledge of Spanish and sign language
~ Ability to conduct accurate eligibility investigations
~ Strong interpersonal, organizational, and interviewing skills
~ Supervisory experience
~ Community relations skills

Experience	Title	Dates
New York Department of Public Aid	Senior Caseworker	1991-1995
Brooklyn Social Services Administration	Caseworker	1987-1991
Brooklyn Department of Veterans' Affairs	Benefits Specialist	1985-1987

Education

New York University	M.S.W.	
Boston College	B.A.	Psychology

References

Available upon request

Grace Miller
615 Robin Lane
Toledo, Ohio
419-555-4803

=================================

Objective: Position as a music therapist

Background: Talented, degreed professional with eight years' experience. Excellent singer, pianist, guitarist. Comfortable with clients/students of all ages and backgrounds. Resourceful and compassionate care and instruction.

Employment: Teaching, counseling, and music therapy positions.

9/89 to Present Rockdale Nursing Center/Toledo, Ohio
        Music Therapist

        *Direct recreational and therapeutic music activities
         at this 500-bed long-term care facility
        *Assess patients' needs
        *Conduct group music activities
        *Perform for patients and staff
        *Arrange for musical presentations by local choirs,
         school groups, and professional musicians

6/89 to 9/89   Toledo Summer Arts/Toledo, Ohio
        Assistant Music Director

        *Assisted music director at this summer camp for young
         musicians
        *Provided information and tours for prospective students
         and their families
        *Designed and supervised group musical activities

           Grace Miller-page 1 of 2

| 9/87 to 6/89 | Shultz Junior High School |
| | Music Teacher |

*Taught music education classes
*Directed choir
*Produced, directed, and publicized large-scale
  holiday performance each year
*Vocal coach for annual variety show

Education:

B.A.   Kenyon College
Major: Music
Minor: Psychology

M.A.   Ohio State University
Major: Music Therapy

References: Will be provided upon request

Grace Miller-page 2 of 2

MARRIETTA SUAREZ
73 Carriage Court
Oklahoma City, OK 73106
(405) 555-5894

CAREER GOAL: *Supervisory position in physical therapy*

EXPERIENCE:

1992-Present   *Oklahoma Rehabilitation Institute*
                 Director, Department of Physical Therapy

   *Supervise ten staff members, including physical therapists, aides,
   and support staff

   *Develop patient therapy programs

   *Attend interdisciplinary staff meetings to coordinate patient care
   with other hospital departments

   *Consult with medical staff as necessary

   *Make recommendations to hospital board regarding departmental
   budget, equipment purchases, facilities design, long-range planning

   *Assist in hiring and training new personnel

1989-1992 Bethany Christian Hospital
           Physical Therapist

   *Assisted stroke and accident victims and other patients in recovery
   of range of motion

   *Provided postoperative physical therapy

   *Assisted patients with adjustment to prosthetic limbs

   *Conducted patient and family education

                         Marietta Suarez-page 1 of 2

1987-1989 McHenry County Veterans Hospital
Physical Therapy Aide

***Assisted physical therapists with all aspects of patient care**

***Extensive charting and recordkeeping**

CREDENTIALS:

Board Certified Physical Therapist, trained at University of Oklahoma

Member, American Physical Therapy Association

REFERENCES:

Will be provided upon request

Marietta Suarez-page 2 of 2

Richard Perkins
1650 Newland Lane
Sioux Falls, SD 57105
(605) 555-7348

Job Experience

*Sioux Falls Police Department   8/89-Present
  Patrolman

Foot patrol, radio car patrol, dispatch officer, special
security assignment at Sioux Falls High School. Police
photographer for accident investigations. Radio
dispatch instructor for new members of force.

Implemented community policing policy. Recognized,
respected member of local community. Received two
Distinguished Service awards.

*Pittsburgh Police Department
  Assistant to Director
  Domestic Violence Unit   8/87-8/89

Handled domestic disturbance calls. Provided community
referral and crisis counseling for families involved.
Filed reports and maintained records. Compiled
statistics. Provided expert and eye witness testimony
in court. Public speaking on issue of domestic violence.

Education

Pennsylvania State Police Academy training course
B.A. in Sociology, University of Pittsburgh

Memberships

Police Athletic League, Sioux Falls
Fraternal Order of Police, Sioux Falls Chapter

References Available on Request

Patricia Kelly
17 Woods Road
Frederick, MD 21702
301-555-3495 (Office)
301-555-3859 (Home)

Background

Experienced academic administrator with demonstrated ability in key areas of financial management, teacher supervision, curriculum development, and community relations.

Administrative Experience

School Superintendant
Frederick , MD
January 1990 to Present

Supervise faculty of 100 teachers. Manage budget of $15 million. Accomplishments include construction of two new elementary schools, implementation of successful bus safety program adopted by other cities, best student/teacher ratio in the state, student test scores in the top 5% of national ratings, ongoing teacher enrichment programs.

Principal
Wakefield Academy
Baltimore, MD
September 1986 to December 1989

Participated in staff hiring, training, and evaluation. Financial management of school, including direction of fundraising efforts. Oversaw curriculum development and textbook adoptions. Interacted with school board, PTA, and community groups. Supervised marketing campaign that increased school enrollment by 7%. Designed inservice programs for teaching staff.

Patricia Kelly-page 1 of 2

Counseling Experience

Guidance Counselor
Bethesda High School
Behesda, MD
September 1983 to June 1986

Provided personal and academic counseling to high school students. As college admissions advisor, arranged college fair that allowed seniors to meet with admissions representatives from 15 colleges. Seventy-five percent of counselees attended first-choice college. Managed work/study program. Designed and implemented Graduation First, a program of personal/academic counseling, flexible scheduling, and work/study options to assist at-risk students and lower the dropout rate.

Teaching Experience

Reading Instructor	*Substitute Teacher*
North Ridge High School	*Clarke County School District*
Bethesda, MD	*Clarke County Maryland*
August 1981 to June 1983	*August 1980 to June 1981*

Education

M.Ed.	*School Administration*	*Univeristy of Virginia*
B.A.	*Education*	*Penn State University*

References

Detailed references will be furnished upon request.

Patricia Kelly-page 2 of 2

Liz Newson   3 Lee Rd.   Santa Barbara, CA 93101
NEWSON ASSOCIATES
Counseling & Alternative Medicine
Phone 805-555-8594
Hours Mon-Fri 8-4 & Evenings by Appointment
~~~~~~~~~~~~~~~~~~~~~~~~~~~~~~

Services:

~Individual and group counseling for personal growth,
 academic progress, health and wellness, career decision
 making and advancement
~Hynotherapy to resolve substance abuse, compulsive
 disorders, and other issues requiring behavioral
 modification
~Relaxation and stress management programs for groups and
 individuals (in my offices or on-site).
~Biofeedback for treatment of stress and sleep disorders
~Acupuncture and herbal treatment for stress management
~Assertiveness training seminars for women

Clients:

```
Consultant          UCLA Department of Psychology
Speaker/Consultant  Triton Wholistic Health Center
Therapist/Owner     Newson Associates
```

Education & Training:

```
M.A. in Clinical Psychology/Western University
B.A. in Psychology, Augustana College
California Acupuncture License
State Certification in Hynotherapy
```

Memberships:

```
American Group Psychotherapy Association
California Mental Health Association
```

References Available

Bruce Wilson
740 Carthage Court
Lake Forest, IL 60045
708-555-4857

Work History

Cook County Juvenile Detention Center   1992-Present
Chicago, Illinois
Educational Director

*Interact with local school districts, social workers, criminal justice officials, and juvenile offenders
*Design group and individual instruction programs
*Hire, train, and evaluate instructors for the program
*Evaluate student progress and adjust curriculum as necessary

Stevenson Youth House   1989-1992
Milwaukee, Wisconsin
Director

*Managed supervised living facility for 20 at-risk adolescent males
*Provided educational and cultural enrichment programs
*Supervised staff of 3
*Responsible for all aspects of financial management
*Provided counseling and employment opportunities for residents

Tacoma Juvenile Correctional Center   1986-1989
Tacoma, Washington
Probation Aide

*Maintained records on juvenile offenders
*Researched case histories and conducted interviews
*Presented written progress reports and recommendations to judicial authorities
*Conducted investigations to assist in apprehension of parole violators

Bruce Wilson-page 1 of 2

Education

Master's Degree	Criminal Justsice	Northern Illinois University
Bachelor's Degree	Education & Psychology	University of Illinois, Champaign

Languages

Fluent in German and Spanish

Conversant in Italian

REFERENCES AVAILABLE

Bruce Wilson-page 2 of 2

John A. Stevens
422 Kenmore Drive
Sarasota, FL 33581
(813) 555-3958

JOB OBJECTIVE: A paramedic position

EXPERIENCE:

Paramedic   Sarasota Fire Department
10/92-Present   Ambulance Rescue Division

Duties: Respond to emergency medical calls. Assess patient's medical condition in field and relay status to hospital emergency staff. Transport patients to area hospitals. Provide basic and advanced life support per physician's phone instructions while enroute to hospital.

Key Skills: vital signs check, CPR, defibrillation, intubation, administration of medication, shock prevention.

EMT   Regency Ambulance Service
1/88-9/92   (private ambulance company)

Duties: Took vital signs and provided basic life support. Transported patients to area hospitals.

Key Skills: Maintenance of airway, provision of oxygen, bleeding control, shock prevention.

EMT   Sarasota General Hospital
5/85-1/88   Emergency Department

Duties: Assisted emergency medical staff in providing direct patient care.

Key Skills: Vital signs check, phlebotomy, EKG.

John A. Stevens-page 1 of 2

EDUCATION:

Sarasota Community College
Associate Degree/Biology

Emergency Medical Technician Courses, I & II

Advanced Cardiac Life Support (ACLS) Certification

CPR Certification

REFERENCES:

Jack Smith   *Sarasota Fire Department*
Fire Chief   *813-555-9845*

Barbara Evans   *Sarasota General Hospital*
Nurse Clinician   *813-555-6735*

Anthony Berelli   *Regency Ambulance Service*
EMT Supervisor   *813-555-7845*

John A . Stevens-page 2 of 2

Mira Suresh
Registered Nurse
1640 Ashfield Road
Nashville, TN 37204
615-555-7896

Employment

United Home Health Care   **(1990-Present)**
Nashville, TN
Registered Nurse

St. Francis Hospital   **(1989-1990)**
Atlanta, GA
Staff Nurse

Davis Family Clinic   **(1986-1989)**
Atlanta, GA
Registered Nurse

Skills

*Home Health Professional: Able to review history, assess patients' needs
 and provide appropriate level of care. Cases have included pediatric through
 geriatric patients. Recent patients have included accident, burn, surgery, stroke,
 heart attack, and AIDS patients. Comfortable using oxygen, IVs, traction, and
 other medical equipment in home setting.

*Experienced Staff Nurse: Responsible for all aspects of patient care. Took
 patient histories, kept charts. Monitored patients' progress, administered
 medications and treatment. Explained procedures and home care to patients
 and their families. Briefed staff on patients' status.

Education

BSN   **University of Georgia**
State Board Certification   **Georgia and Tennessee**

REFERENCES AVAILABLE

James Kearns
450 Merrill Drive
Ann Arbor, MI 48106
(313) 555-8965

Career Goal: Position in elementary education

Experience

Woodland Elementary School, Ann Arbor, MI, 1990-Present
Fifth Grade Teacher

*Responsible for classes of 20-25 fifth graders for past five years
*Teach core curriculum: math, English, science, and social science
*Work with music, art, and other teachers to coordinate curriculum
*Administer national academic progress tests
*Teacher representative on district's curriculum review board
*Organize and direct annual science fair

Jefferson Elementary School, Ann Arbor, MI, 1988-1990

*Responsible for fourth grade classes of 18-22 students
*Taught core curriculum
*Participated in long-range curriculum planning, reviewing
 such issues as textbook adoptions and combined classroom concept
*Organized fundraising drive to fund expanded computer learning
 center, including candy sales and direct community fundraising
*Organized and supervised field trips

Education

M.A.   Rice University   Michigan Certification
       Houston, Texas
       Elementary Education   Grades 1-6
B.S.   Ohio State University
       Columbus, Ohio
       Education/Biology

Professional Affiliations

          National Education Association
          Parent Teachers Association
          Michigan Teachers Association

References are available upon request

WARREN DEVEROE
118 W. 86th Street, #3C
New York, NY 10024
(212) 555-4960

Specialization

Nonprofit fundraising and marketing consultant

Capabilities

~ Experienced in all aspects of direct mail campaigns
~ Design, write, and produce informational and fundraising letters
  and brochures
~ Manage telemarketing campaigns
~ Conduct market research
~ Write press releases for radio, TV, newspapers, and magazines
~ Degrees in business and marketing
~ Eight years as successful business consultant

Clients

*National Public Radio   *Mothers Against Drunk Drivers
*World Wildlife Federation   *Cancer Federation
*Special Olympics   *Americans for International Aid

Education

Queens College   Villanova University
B.S./Business Marketing   M.B.A./Financial Management

References

Will be furnished upon request

Lisa Denorelli
1611 Margaret Street
Scranton, PA 18505
(717) 555-4983 (Office)
(717) 555-4094 (Home)

Objective	Management of nonprofit social service agency
Current Position	Director, Susan's Place, Scranton , PA 1992-Present Community Social Service Agency for Women

General manager of local women's center providing the following services:

*Legal Aid	*Food Pantry
*Day Care	*Homeless Shelter
*Job Training	*Counseling &Referral

Duties include:

*Bookkeeping	*Community Outreach
*Staffing	*Fundraising
*Program Design	*Long-range Planning

Previous Positions	AIDS Action Committee, Pittsburgh, PA Media Specialist 1989-1992
	Children's Welfare League, New York, NY Fundraiser 1988-1989
	Center for Domestic Violence Research, New York, NY Researcher 1986-1988
Education	M.S.W. University of Massachusetts, Amherst B.A. English / Simmons College, Boston, MA
References	Available on Request

Darrell Simpson
60 Stevens Parkway
Cincinnati, Ohio 45242
(513) 555-0979

Objective

Position with a recreation or social service agency that will allow me to
continue to serve youth.

Work History

Outward Bound Cincinnati, OH Program Director 1994-Present

Organize and supervise trips (one day to one week) for teens. Program
teaches wilderness survival skills, self-reliance, self-esteem, group
interdependence. Arrange all aspects of trips, including assisting
with advertising, scouting locations and preparing sites, supervising
registration and transportation, designing and directing activities.
Recruit and train new volunteers. Expanded program participation 15%.

The Wilderness Society Seattle, WA Youth Coordinator 1991-1994

Developed program of nature appreciation and conservancy for children
and teens. Designed Outdoor Adventure, guided walks at area nature
preserves for elementary students. Coordinated with National Park
Service to set up education centers at two local parks. Led Wilderness
Teen Camp backpacking, canoeing, and camping trips designed to
improve fitness, self-confidence, and environmental awareness.

Camp Wichita Wichita, KS Activities Director 1989-1991

Designed and supervised on-site recreational activities and day trips
for over 120 campers ages 5 to 10. Trained, supervised, and
evaluated counselors.

Education/Certifications

B.A. Leisure & Recreation Western Illinois University
Red Cross First Aid and Swimming Certifications

References Available

Rhonda Leventhal
16 Easton Court
Salt Lake City, UT 84116
(801) 555-9987

Professional Experience

Wee Care Day School   *Owner/Operator*
420 Rose Lane   *1992-Present*
Salt Lake City, UT

Own and operate day care center serving up to 25 children, ages 1-5 years. Direct staff of 4 in providing routine care, educational development opportunities, and social interaction for children. Center is housed in a modern facility with fully equipped nap center, changing station, classroom/playroom, outdoor play area andsmall lunchroom. Staff includes 3 highly qualified teachers and office manager. Excellent record of safety and customer satisfaction. Client list available.

Child Care Program   *Assistant Director*
NUA Business Systems   *1990-1992*
4833 Industrial Parkway
Salt Lake City, UT

Assistant to director of on-site day care center operated for employees of NUA. Interacted with children, teachers, parents, and company management to meet the needs of 40 children in full-day and before/after school programs. Organized and directed activities. Administered routine care, and first aid as necessary.

Rhonda Leventhal-page 1 of 2

Kensington Montessori School   **Teacher's Aide**
5130 Kensington Court   **1989-1990**
Salt Lake City, UT

Assisted preschool teacher at local Montessori school. Conducted games and activities designed to improve children's fine motor skills, self-expression, social skills, and educational preparedness. Participated in teacher/parent conferences and staff meetings.

Professional Credentials

Associate Degree   **Early Childhood Education**
Salt Lake City Community College

Licensed Child Care Worker
Utah Board of Commissioners

CPR/First Aid Certification

Member in Good Standing
National Association of Child Care Professionals

References

Detailed references will be furnished upon request.

Rhonda Leventhal-page 2 of 2

ROBERT ELLISON
414 Jefferson Street
New Orleans, LA 70119

SUMMARY

Environmental scientist with ten years' experience. Have held both private sector and government agency positions.

CAPABILITIES

Experienced in visual inspection and chemical analysis of suspicious effluents

Comprehensive knowledge of EPA methods and procedures

Detailed understanding of state industrial pollution and toxin standards

Experience in land management and reclamation research

Project management and supervisory experience

EMPLOYERS

Environmental Defense Fund Staff Environmentalist	(1993-Present)
U.S. Environmental Protection Agency Environmentalist III	(1989-1993)
United Chemical Corporation Environmental Consultant	(1986-1989)
Louisiana Department of Fish & Wildlife Field Inspector II	(1984-1986)

EDUCATION

B.S.   Chemistry   University of Illinois, Chicago

References   Available Upon Request

Amy Ryan
1450 Magnolia Lane
Lemon Grove, California 92045
(805) 555-5678

Nonprofit Public Information Specialist

Goal

Public information position in nonprofit health care organization
that utilizes my strong writing and public relations skills

Work History

American Cancer Society, Goletta, California
Public Information Specialist   1992-Present

Design, write, and produce major publications including monthly
newsletter, annual report, and fundraising brochures. Write
press releases and act as liaison between ACS and media, including
newspapers, television, and radio journalists. Arrange press
conferences at request of Public Information Director.

Parkland General Hospital, Ventura, California
Public Information Intern   1991-1992

Wrote and edited press releases for local mediaa. Developed,
researched, and wrote articles for quarterly magazine. Wrote and
edited speeches for hospital board members. Produced copy and
aquired photos for fundraising brochures.

Education

B.A. Degree/Public Relations
University of California
Los Angeles, California

References

Available on Request

Helena Shapiro
86 Wayland Court
Boulder, CO 80205
(303) 555-9085

Experience

Denver Museum of Art   1993-Present
Docent and Educator

Conduct educational tours of museum for elementary grades. Direct
Young Masters Program, summer and weekend courses in drawing,
painting, and sculpture for gifted students.

Private Art Teacher   **1990-1995**

Offer private instruction in painting and drawing from my home studio. Specialize
in students ages 5-15.

Richardson Elementary School   **1990-1993**
Art Teacher

Taught art education courses to grades K-6. Organized art contests within school
and student submissions to district and statewide contests. Assisted students
in producing sets and props for annual variety show. Interacted with students,
staff, teachers, parents, and PTA.

Education

B.A.   Art History/Elementary Education
University of Colorado, Boulder, Colorado

References Available

KEVIN PAULSON
715 Conway Court
Santa Fe, NM 85702
(505) 555-4958

<u>Skills Summary</u>

Athletic Training/Coaching

*Personal Trainer/Valley Fitness Center/Santa Fe

  Designed individual fitness programs that were safe yet
  challenging. Motivated clients to continue with fitness regimen.

*Basketball Coach/Santa Fe Community High School/Santa Fe

  Coach high school basketball team with winning record in conference.
  Determine strategy, teach players specific formations and general
  skills. Provide psychological motivation. Supervise team during
  games. Good rapport with players, officials, school administrators,
  and parents. Emphasis on developing fitness and good sportsmanship.

Teaching

*Physical Education Teacher/Santa Fe Community High School/Santa Fe

  Teach boys' PE courses. Responsible for teaching diverse core
  curriculum, including swimming, baseball, basketball, tennis, and
  volleyball. Assist athletic director with schoolwide fitness
  testing program

*Aerobics Instructor/Valley Fitness Center/Santa Fe

  Taught both low- and high-impact aerobics. Designed routines and
  selected music. Taught students self-monitoring skills to ensure a safe
  workout.

Other

*Experienced lifeguard and swimming instructor

                              Kevin Paulson-page 1 of 2

Employers

```
Santa Fe Community High School, Santa Fe   1992-1995
Valley Fitness Center, Santa Fe            1989-1992
Community Swim Center, Santa Barbara, CA   Summers/1985-1989
```

Education

B.A./Physical Education/University of California/Santa Barbara
Secondary Teaching Certification/New Mexico and California
Red Cross Certified Swimming Instructor

References

References will be furnished upon request.

Kevin Paulson-page 2 of 2

Jessica Erickson
83 Silver Spring Road
Anchorage, AK 99503
(907) 555-5960

SUMMARY

Private psychotherapist with successful practice for past five years. Previous experience in health care and business settings. Proven record of success at teaching clients behavioral modification techniques. Training and experience with 12-step system. Individual and group therapy.

PROFESSIONAL SKILLS

~ Experience dealing with eating disorders, including anorexia nervosa, bulimia, and morbid obesity

~ Substance abuse strategies, including 12-step methods and suppport groups for alcohol and drug addiction recovery

~ Crisis counseling and interventions for families of substance abusers

~ Referral to appropriate community and health care services as necessary

~ Track progress and coordinate counseling and recovery strategies for patients hospistalized for treatment

~ Public speaking engagements to address issues of substance abuse and eating disorders

EDUCATION

M.A.	Clinical Psychology	University of Alaska, Anchorage
B.A.	Sociology	Alaska Pacific University

Jessica Erickson-page 1 of 2

EMPLOYMENT HISTORY

1990-1995   **Private Practice**   **Anchorage, AK**

1987-1990   **Counselor**
                   Bristol Clinic   **Anchorage, AK**
                   (private clinic for substance
                     abuse recovery)

1986-1987   **Counselor**
                   Diet Center Inc.   **Juneau, AK**

REFERENCES

References will be furnished on request.

Jessica Erickson-page 2 of 2

Hannah Colgan/Counselor
4215 Ridge Road
Washington, D.C. 90210
(212) 555-3959

Areas of Expertise
~ ~ ~ ~ ~ ~ ~ ~

Residential counseling for at-risk adolescents

Grief therapy for clients recovering from a death, divorce, or other loss

Marital counseling and conflict resolution techniques

Crisis counseling and treatment of clinical depression

Chemical dependency assessment and treatment

Eating disorder assessment and treatment

Education and Training
~ ~ ~ ~ ~ ~ ~ ~ ~ ~ ~ ~

B.A.	Psychology	Georgetown University, Washington, D.C.
M.A.	Counseling	University of Wisconsin, Madison, Wisconsin
Certificate	Grief Therapy	Loyola College, Montreal

Work History
~ ~ ~ ~ ~ ~

| Brookside Group Home Washington, DC | Consultant 1992-Present |

Mental health consultant to residential program for adolescents at risk. Consult with staff members on cases as requested. Conduct group therapy sessions for emotionally troubled teens. Attend monthly staff meetings. Participate in fundraising efforts and long-range planning.

Hannah Colgan-page 1 of 2

Wilson, Colgan & Stevenson   **Therapist/Co-Owner**
Mental Health Associates   **1990-Presesnt**
Washington, DC

Partner in private menal health practice. Current patient load of 60+ patients in ongoing individual and group therapy dealing with personal, marital, substance abuse, and other issues. Monitor and record patient progress. Attend weekly staff meeting. Provide referral services.

Conlin Clinic   **Substance Abuse Specialist**
Bethesda, MD   **1987-1990**

Took patient histories and assessed patient needs. Provided details of substance abuse program to patients and families. Conducted tours of facility for prospective patients and families. Helped patients adjust to clinic. Provided individual and group counseling. Monitored patient progress, assisted patients with discharge planning. Instituted family support group.

Community Service
~ ~ ~ ~ ~ ~ ~ ~ ~

St. Paul's Suicide Prevention Hotline
Washington, DC   **Volunteer**

Nicolet Mental Health Center   **Member**
Bethesda, MD   **Board of Directors**

References Available
~ ~ ~ ~ ~ ~ ~ ~ ~

Timothy Vaughn
450 King Drive
Bennington, CT 48009
(203) 555-5948

WORK HISTORY

<u>Landscape Architect</u>   City of Bennington, CT   1990-Present

Design public parks and recreational areas within the city

Work with government and community groups to coordinate preservation efforts and address environmental concerns

Research land use and provide written reports to city government

Provide project suggestions and estimated budgets to city planning officials

Supervise routine park maintenance and park enhancement projects

Purchase park maintenance equipment

<u>Supervisor</u>   Grove Nursery, Montgomery, AL   1987-1990

Hired, trained, and supervised nursery staff

Selected subcontractors and negotiated prices and delivery schedules

Purchased and maintained all equipment

Supervised landscaping projects for clients, including ground maintenance and installation of gardens, borders, and annual displays

EDUCATION

B.S.   Landscape Architecture   University of Alabama
            Licensed Landscape Contractor

        REFERENCES AVAILABLE

Yolanda Ortega
655 Ashland Drive
Irvine, California 92714
(714) 555-9587

Objective: *Social service position with supervisory potential*

Employment:

1993-Present	*Caseworker*	*Los Angeles County Social Services*
1991-1993	*Medical Social Worker*	*Los Angeles Office of Veterans Affairs*
1987-1991	*Administrative Assistant*	*Los Angeles County Legal Aid Society*

Education

B.A.	*Sociology*	*University of California, Santa Barbara, California*

Skills

*Research applicants' eligibility for social services and approve or deny claims
*Manage large caseloads in timely and compassionate manner in accordance with
  agency guidelines
*Interview social service applicants and inform them of their rights and
  responsibilities
*Provide referral to other community agencies as appropriate
*Bilingual--Spanish/English--able to translate legal and other complex
  documents and interpret for hispanic clients
*Excellent clerical and organizational skills
*Knowledge of WordPerfect, Microsoft Word, and Lotus 1-2-3

References

Cecilia Reed   Senior Caseworker   *L.A. Office of Veterans Affairs*
(213) 555-5068

Michael Wu   Attorney   *L.A. Legal Aide Society*
(213)555-6079

Martin O'Connor
433 North Street
Easton, CT 06612
(203) 555-5906

Objective

Retail pharmacy position with supervisory responsibility

Pharmacy Experience

Retail Pharmacist   Star Drugs, Easton, CT
1991-Present

Manage retail drug store. Duties include purchase of drugs and
sundries, customer service, consultation with physicians,
patient education on drug use and interactions, supervision of
assistant. Computerized pharmacy. Increased sales by 50%.

Pharmacy Assistant   Brady Pharmacy, Champaign, IL
1988-1990

Assistant to local pharmacist as part of internship program.
Basic customer service and delivery of medication.
Prescription data entry under supervision of pharmacist.

Education

Bachelor of Pharmacy, University of Illinois, Champaign, Illinois

References

Will be provided upon request

Gregory Sansone
17 Sandstone Court
Augusta, Georgia 30901
(404) 555-9684

Employment

July 1990 *to* *September 1995*	*Deputy Sheriff, Augusta, Georgia* *General law enforcement duties, including supervision of police officers and staff, traffic control, accident investigation, crowd control, cooperation with state and federal authorities on criminal investigations.*
January 1987 *to* *June 1990*	*Detective, Atlanta Police Department* *Responsible for electronic and other surveillance of criminal suspects, including pursuit of suspects and documentation of their whereabouts, evidence collection. Knowledge of video and photo surveillance. Familiar with pertinent civil and criminal statutes.*
September 1986 *to* *December 1986*	*Special Investigator, Atlanta Police Department* *Hired on temporary basis to assist with undercover drug investigation. Assisted officers with surveillance. Provided courtroom testimony for investigation leading to four arrests and convictions.*
Education	*B.S. Criminal Justice* *Illinois State University* *Atlanta Police Training Institute*
Certification	*Evidence Technician* *Narcotics Investigation* *Surveillance Techniques*

References Available Upon Request

Edith Kravitz

4820 Briarcrest Drive   Richmond, VA 23226   (804) 555-4859

Specialization   Academic Counseling

Work History

Guidance Counselor
North Central High School
Richmond, Virginia
1991-1995

Resident Counselor
Calrendon Academy
Richmond, Virginia
1989-1991

English Teacher
Grant High School
Midlothian, Virginia
1986-1989

English Teacher
Emporia High School
Emporia, Virginia
1984-1986

Skills

~ Admissions and financial aid advice for college-bound juniors and seniors
~ Curriculum counseling for high school students
~ Organization and supervision of work/study programs
~ Individual and group counseling for adolescents to resolve personal problems and improve academic performance
~ Study skills, college selection, and resume/job search seminars for students
~ Resident advisor for adolescents
~ Experienced English instructor

Accomplishments

~ Reduced dropout rate at North Central High (15% during last four years)
~ Increased student and community business involvement in work/study program
~ Awarded PTA Excellence in Education Award 1994

Edith Kravitz-page 1 of 2

Education

B.A.
English
Boston College

M.Ed.
Guidance & Counseling
University of New Hampshire

Certified School Guidance Counselor
State of Virginia Board of Education

References

Marsha Pell, Director
Clarendon Academy
(804) 555-2839

Walter Davis,Principal
North Central High School
(804) 555-3958

Edith Kravitz-page 2 of 2

KEVIN LEE
1015 Rialto Street
Bennington, VT 05201

Objective: Hospital Administration

PROFESSIONAL EXPERIENCE

Financial Management

*Experience preparing and managing annual budgets of up to $15 million
*Fundraising ability, including soliciting corporate funds and private donation
 to fund hospital expansion projects
*Cost-effective resolution of woker's compensation claims, employee
 contracts, and rate negotiation with insurance companies
*Administration of successful materials cost containment program that has
 reduced expenditures for hospital supplies by approximately 20%

Personnel Management

*Development of ongoing nursing recruitment program that increased staffing
 to 95% of required level, with full staffing expected within the next year
*Implementation of successful community volunteer program
*Successful labor negotiations and reduction in staff turnover rate of 15%
*Extensive staff development programs and opportunities. Strong
 commitment to continuing education of staff

Marketing and Administration

*Maintenance of professional standards as evidenced by full accreditation of
 both hospitals during tenure
*Direction of successful public information and marketing programs
*Facilities maintenance and planning, including expansion and updating of
 hospital facilities

Kevin Lee-page 1 of 2

EDUCATION

Columbia University		Georgetown University	
B.A.	Economics	M.S.	Hospital Administration

AFFILIATIONS

Consultant, President's Task Force on Health Care Reform
American Hospital Association
American Society of Hospital Administrators

EMPLOYMENT

Bennington Memorial Hospital	Georgetown General Hospital
Bennington, Vermont	Washington, D.C.
1992-Present	1987-1992

REFERENCES

References will be provided on request

Kevin Lee-page 2 of 2

MICHAEL WINTERS
304 Harrison Street
Brooklyn, New York 11213
Office 212-555-7609
Home 212-555-4059

CAREER GOAL   Management of nonprofit social service agency

WORK HISTORY

Position: **Director, AIDS Action Coalition**
                     Brooklyn, New York
                     1991-1995

Skills Used: *Financial Management   *Public Education
                     *Fundraising   *Governmental Lobbying
                     *Research   *Public Speaking

Direct the agency as it pursues the goal of achieving public sensitivity to AIDs
and adequate funding for treatment and research. Manage staff of 10employees
and 30 volunteers. Direct fundraising efforts. Publish monthly newsletter.
Interact with other community service and health care organizations striving
to meet the needs of persons living with AIDS. Monitor pertinent state and
federal legislation and organize lobbying efforts.   Public speaking engagements.

Position: **Director, Nessett House**
                     Brooklyn, New York
                     1989-1991

Skills Used: *Fundraising   *Substance Abuse Therapy
                     *Financial Management   *Group Therapy
                     *Community Outreach   *Conflict Resolution

Resident director at supervised living facility serving residents recovering from
substance abuse and alcohol addiction. Management of budget and direction of
day-to-day operations. Direction of publicity efforts and fundraising campaigns.
Provision of individual and group substance abuse recovery counseling.

Michael Winters-page 1 of 2

EDUCATION

B.A.	**Rutgers University**	
	Economics and Psychology	
M.S.W.	**Boston University**	
	Counseling & Psychology	
Coursework	**New York University**	
	Accounting	

REFERENCES

Will be provided upon request

Michael Winters-page 2 of 2

SHEILA RYAN
73 Wisconsin Street
Portland, OR 97219
Phone 503-555-3958

<u>Objective:</u> A responsible position as a political aide

<u>Key Skills:</u>   *Fundraising   *Speech Writing
                *Publicity   *Office Management
                *Public Speaking   *Research

<u>Job Experience:</u>

Office of Congresswoman Mary Martin/Office Manager/1993 to Present

*Compile statistics and write weekly status reports
*Attend staff meetings
*Supervise office staff, including training, scheduling, and evaluation
*Draft responses to constituents' letters
*Assist with fundraising efforts
*Write and present speeches on congresswoman's policies to women's
 and community groups

Office of Assemblyman Walter Smith/Office Assistant/1990-1993

*Responded to constituents' concerns
*Heavy telephone and correspondence duties
*Wrote campaign brochure and press releases

<u>Volunteer Work:</u>

League of Women Voters/Assistant to Educational Director/1989-1990
Amnesty International/Active Member /1989-Present

<u>Education:</u>

B.S.   University of Wisconsin/Madison
              Political Science Major

REFERENCES ON REQUEST

Elizabeth Anne Engle
16 N. Sheffield Road
Minneapolis, MN 55429
(612) 555-4744

Professional Goal: To utilize my nursing skills in a challenging position in a
professional health care setting

Professional Strengths:

* Proven ability to assist patients and families in developing
  appropriate coping strategies in response to illness

* Strong assessment skills for evaluating patients' needs and
  providing proper referrals to other medical professionals
  and community support groups

* Successful experience mediating between staff members and
  acting as community liaison

* Strong commitment to continuing education and patient advocacy

Education:

BSN, Marywood College, 1990
MSN, Community Health, College of Misericordia, 1994

Previous Positions:

Nursing Consultant, Swedish American Hospice, 1993-Present
Pediatric Staff Nurse, Shriners Children's Hospital, 1990-1993

References Available on Request

Amanda Richardson
915 Lake Street, #6B
White Plains, NY 10036
(914) 555-7934

Excellent eight-year record of service to the city of White Plains, New York, in their uniform division. Helped implement community policing policy credited with reducing local crime rate.

ACHIEVEMENTS

White Plains Police Department (1987-1995)

*Conducted successful robbery and assault investigations leading to approximately 40 arrests.

*Interviewed both suspects and complaintants.

*Conducted background checks.

*Organized and participated in community safety awareness programs at local schools and businesses.

*Orientation supervisor for new officers.

AWARDS

3 Distinguished Service Awards (1992,1993,1995)
Mayor's Community Service Award (1993)
Certificate of Service, White Plains School District 84 (1995)

EDUCATION

B.A. Degree * Law & Society
University of California, Los Angeles

New York State Police Academy
Graduated with Honors

REFERENCES AVAILABLE UPON REQUEST

Johanna Brown
133 Lincoln Drive
Detroit, MI 48099
(613) 555-3361

POSITION DESIRED	Health Care Administrator in a hospital or clinic.
EDUCATION	Master of Science Degree, April, 1972, Western Michigan University, Public Health Administration. Bachelor of Science Degree, April, 1968, Western Michigan University. Major: Business. Minor: Biology.
EXPERIENCE	1972-1993: Director, Vicksburg Community Hospitals. Responsible for the operation of the entire hospital: financial planning, personnel, medical activities, and plant. 1971-1972: Assistant Director, Vicksburg Community Hospitals. Handled inpatient and outpatient admittance, cost control, and emergency services. 1968-1971: Assistant Director, Plainwell Community Hospitals. Managed billing practices, cost control, and new cost procedures.
COMMUNITY SERVICE	Volunteer Firefighter in Vicksburg, 8 years. Member of the committee to study the emergency care facilities in Vicksburg.
RELEVANT INFORMATION	Participated in professional in-service seminars such as: cost control, financial planning, billing and collection systems, inpatient admittance, and Lynn Hall's lecture series relating Occupational Therapy to the hospital environment. Member of the American Public Health Association and American Academy of Hospital Administrators.

Chapter Six

SAMPLE COVER LETTERS

Salavador Mendez
6431 North Sheridan Road,
#2B
Chicago, Illinois 60626

August 26, 1995

Ms. Kathryn Chambers
Human Resources
Rollins Family Center
206 N. Kolmar Avenue
Chicago, Illinois 60624

Dear Ms. Chambers:

Kindly consider me an applicant for the position of Assistant Outreach Director as advertised in Sunday's <u>Chicago Tribune</u>. The enclosed resume outlines some of my qualifications for this job.

Your advertisement states that applicants should have a Master's degree in social work and at least three years of experience in individual and family therapy. In addition, you are looking for someone who is "knowledgeable about substance and alcohol abuse and who is sensitive to the social and cultural needs of a diverse population." I believe you will find that my background matches these requirements.

I have four years experience as a crisis intervention social worker at Lutheran General Hospital. Approximately one-third of the cases I have managed have been directly related to substance and/or alcohol abuse. As a doctoral student at the Institute for Clinical Social Work, I have focused my research on substance

Page Two
Salavador Mendez

abuse and am currently preparing my manuscript, <u>Effective Psychotherapy for Substance Abusers</u>, for publication. It includes twenty specific case studies with detailed long- and short-term counseling strategies as well as information regarding family and community support services.

The patients I counsel in the emergency room and medical clinic represent the diverse population of the Chicago area. I have concentrated my outreach involvement in the Hispanic community and have coordinated Lutheran General's efforts for early intervention therapy through the Howard Avenue Clinic. I am also familiar with the Rollins Family Center and the multicultural community it serves. I have consulted with several of your staff members, including Maria Gonzalez and Dr. Phillip Meyers, whose clients have been admitted to Lutheran General.

I would welcome the opportunity to meet with you to further discuss my qualifications for the position of Assistant Outreach Director. You can contact me at (312) 555-8623 or at (312) 555-3158. I look forward to hearing from you.

Respectfully,

Salvador Mendez

Elizabeth Anne Engle
16 N. Sheffield Road
Minneapolis, MN 55429

March 21, 19__

Mr. Walter Howards
Director of Staff Development
St. Mary's Children's Hospital
2346 Bloomington Avenue
Minneapolis, MN 55404

Dear Mr. Howards:

I am writing in response to your recent advertisement in the
<u>Minneapolis Star</u>. The postion of Case Manager at St. Mary's
Children's Hospital seems to be a perfect match to my career
objectives, and my professional qualifications appear to meet all
of your requirements. I would appreciate the opportunity to
discuss my credentials for this position with you during a
personal interview.

Your ad states that you are seeking an "MSN with strong
professional background in patient advocacy and family support
services." As a Nursing Consultant for the past three years at
Swedish-American Hospice, I have provided long-term assistance to
more than one hundred patients and their families. I designed the
current program of family support services at the hospice which
has been used as a model for three other long-term care centers in
Minnesota. I supervise six patient advocates and provide
mandatory training in the area of patients rights to all new
medical personnel at Swedish-American.

My experience as a pediatric staff nurse at Shriner's Children's
Hospital has made me sensitive to the particular needs of children
and their families in times of medical crisis. I would welcome
the chance to combine my nursing and advocacy skills in the field
of pediatrics.

I can be reached on a confidential basis during the day at (612)
555-3674 or in the evenings at my home number (612) 555-4744.
Thank you for your consideration.

Sincerely,

Elizabeth Anne Engle

Greg Simon
947 W. Harwood Road
Lawrenceburg, IN 47025

July 6, 19_

Mr. Robert Gilmore
Lawrenceburg Sports Club
1502 Prospect Drive
Lawrenceburg, IN 47025

Dear Mr. Gilmore:

My supervisor, Captain James Willes, suggested that I contact you regarding a possible opening for a firearms instructor at the Lawrenceburg Sports Club. I hope that after reviewing the enclosed resume you will agree that I have the training and professional dedication to qualify to teach at your club.

I have served honorably with the Lawrenceburg Police Department for two years. My firearms certifications include Special Weapons and Tactics and Indiana State Firearms Instructing. As an International Firearms Instructors Organization member, I meet with other police officers to discuss ways to improve firearms safety and education. I also help draf the organization's teaching guidelines. To date, I have led three firearm training courses. I am dedicated to providing qualityfirearms instruction and am certain you share this goal.

I would enjoy meeting with you to discuss the prospect of employment at the Lawrenceburg Sports Club and our mutual goal of firearm safety.

Sincerely,

Greg Simon

Soo-Mi Chay
28 Elm Street
Brockton, MA 02403

November 6, 19___

Ms. Joyce Maynard
Hillside Women's Correctional Center
18 Harris Street
Boston, MA 02109

Dear Ms. Maynard:

A mutual friend of ours, Roberta Sinclair, suggested that I contact you. Roberta was a student at Mount Holyoke College while I was the director of the college career center. I provided her with career counseling in her junior and senior years, and after graduation she returned to volunteer as my assistant. When I made the decision to open my own business, Roberta was chosen as my successor. Since then, we have remained close friends and colleagues. She tells me that you are looking for someone to conduct career counseling seminars for inmates who are approaching release. I have enclosed my resume to give you an indication of my experience int his field and would appreciate the opportunity to meet with you to discuss my qualifications in more detail.

For the past five years, I have provided career counseling to more thantwo hundred individuals. This has included assessing clients' career strengths, planning job search strategies, and motivating individuals to maximize their potential. I have

Page Two

counseled corporate groups as large as 250. When the Atlas Paper Company closed its Brockton plant in 1994 and had to lay off over a hundred employees, the director of personnel hired me to help these workers seek new jobs. I have also worked as a consultant for the United Standard Insurance Company and Brighton Business Associates.

I have a particular interest in helping women develop comprehensive plans for self-improvement through successful job placement. I developed and presented seminars at the Gove Street Women's Center and the Brockton Community Center for women returning to the workforce..

I hope that you will contact me at my office, (508) 555-6843, at your earliest convenience. I am looking forward to meeting you; Roberta has told me a great deal about you.

Sincerely,

Soo-Mi Chay

Allan A. MacFarlan
5448 W. Fournier Road
Westerly, RI 02891

March 16, 19__

Wilkes-Jacob Incorporated
ATTN: SB/LIB
64 Michigan Avenue
Washington, D.C. 20010

Dear Colleagues:

Wilkes-Jacob Incorporated's reputation as a key
provider of library services to the federal government
has inspired me to investigate obtaining a position
with your company. I am interested in putting my
proven library skills to work in a setting where I can
assist patrons with research projects and advance my
professional growth. Please consider the enclosed
resume for any current or future openings.

As head librarian at Providence College for six years,
I was responsible for a collection of 680,000 volumes
housed in four separate libraries. During my tenure,
120,000 volumes were added, and the cataloguing system
was updated and automated. I supervised a staff of
nine assistant librarians and over thirty student
workers and volunteers. I am experienced in on-line
searches and information retrieval using databases such
as Dialog and Lexis.

I am planning to move to Washington, D.C. next month
and would enjoy discussing my qualifications with you
when I arrive, or earlier should you have an immediate
opening. I can be reached at (401) 555-4186 until
April 26. After that, contact me at (703) 555-2164.

Thank you for considering my credentials.

Sincerely,

Allan A. MacFarlan

Mary A. Griffin
102 Edgewater Court
Easton, PA 18042

November 2, 19___

Ms. Jane Kennedy
St. Clair Hospital
100 Bower Hill Road
Pittsburgh, PA 15243

Dear Ms. Kennedy:

I am seeking a responsible position within a senior care center dedicated to meeting the needs of the elderly. I understand that St. Clair Hospital is seeking an experienced public relations specialist/fundraiser for part-time employment. After considering my resume, I think you will agree that I am the right person for this job.

For fifteen years as the director of the Easton Community Senior Center, I was responsible for all aspects of the center's operations. The center had more than two hundred registered members, five full-time staffers, and thirty volunteers. During my tenure, I increased the budget by 80%, 90% of which came from grant proposals and fund-raising activities. By publishing a monthly newsletter and articles for the local newspapers, I generated interest in and financial support of the center. I also met regularly with members of the Easton Business Association to solicit contributions for the center.

I would like the opportunity to discuss specific fund-raising activities with you. I am sure my experiences at the Easton Senior Center could be applied with the same positive results at St. Clair's Senior Center. I look forward to hearing from you.

Sincerely,

Mary A. Griffin

Janet K. Shafer
1026 River Road
Columbia, MO 65201

March 24, 19___

Michael Johnson
Personnel Department
St. Luke's Institute
Beachview Drive
Columbia, MO 65203

Dear Mr. Johnson:

Enclosed please find my resume in response to your
advertisement in the <u>Columbia Democrat</u> for a Social
Worker/Psychotherapist. This position is very much in line
with my current career objective, and I believe you will find
my qualifications meet all of your requirements.

Your advertisement calls for a state-licensed social worker
who has experience wih substance abuse populations.
From 1990 to 1993, I worked as an addiction therapist at
Holy Cross Hospital. My responsibilities included assessing
clients' needs, organizing comprehensive treatment plans,
and developing educational programs and materials. In
addition, I counseled family members in group sessions and
provided individual treatment for adult children of alcoholics.
During my two years as a crisis therapist at Boone Hospital
Center, I have continued to work with clients with
substance or alcohol addictions. Many of the crises I have
encountered in the hospital emergency room are the result
of alcohol and/or other substance abuse.

2.

Although my work at the Boone Hospital Center has been challenging and rewarding, I am interested in working in a small psychiatric hospital as a member of an interdisciplinary treatment team. I would like to help develop program planning and to work with clients in a long-term, complete care addiction center.

Please contact me at my office, (314) 555-3786, or in the evenings at my home number, (314) 555-1678. I am anxious to discuss my background and the specifics of this position.

Sincerely,

Janet K. Schafer

TO: Margo Wilkins
Director
Austin Youth Center
Easton, PA 18042

FROM: David Swanson
650 Clifton Avenue
Austin, TX 68143
(612) 555-6915

DATE: April 3, 19___

RE: Opening for Recreational Director

Studies have shown that the safest, most prosperous communities are those that provide adequate educational and recreational opportunities for their citizens. Community centers for youth such as the Austin Youth Center enhance the lives of young adults and keep the community safe. My current position as director of the adult education program for High School District 84, and my previous experiences with Head Start and Outward Bound, have increased my personal commitment to education and recreational social services. I would welcome the opportunity to design educational and recreational programs for your clients and am therefore submitting the enclosed resume in response to your recent advertisement in the *Austin Journal*.

As my resume indicates, I am skilled in the areas of supervision, program design and organization, communications, and teaching. I currently supervise a highly successful work/study program for the high school district that has increased the high school completion rate by 20% over the last five years. During my tenure with Head Start in Atlanta, I established course objectives, designed curriculum, and successfully lobbied for funding. In 1989 I was awarded the Atlanta Community Service Medal.

I believe my credentials are a good match for your current needs. The quality of services at the Austin Youth Center is impressive, and I would enjoy the challenge of serving as your recreational director.

Thank you for your consideration of my qualifications. I would welcome the opportunity discuss the position in person.

Velio A. Pansera
8145 Oketo Avenue
Niles, IL 60714
(708) 555-7102

April 11, 19 __

Mr. Walter Holt
Principal
Maple School
543 Center Street
Des Plaines, IL 60016

Dear Mr. Holt:

Today's *Tribune* advertisement indicates that you are seeking a school psychologist. I believe the credentials and enthusiasm I would bring to such a position will interest you.

As the enclosed resume indicates, I have Type 73 Certification and diverse experience working with children and young adults. In addition to my experiene in psychology and education, I have coached softball and volleyball.

My strongest asset is my ability to provide effective academic and behavioral assistance to students. My skills include:

*Administering and interpreting psychological and educational diagnostic tests.

*Leading ongoing individual and family counseling sessions.

*Training classroom teachers in the use of effective behavior modification techniques.

If you agree that my qualifications suit your needs, I am available at your convenience for a personal interview.

Sincerely,

Velio A. Pansera

Christina A. Rivera
607 Ramsey Drive
Arlington, VA 22209

May 2, 19___

Lincolnwood Elementary School
P.O. Box 64
Richmond, VA 68712

Dear Colleagues:

I am extremely interested in the special education opening for next fall which you announced in last Sunday's <u>Richmond Gazette.</u> My skills and experience seem to be exactly what you seek to serve the special education students at Lincoln Elementary School.

I recently acquired my M.Ed. at the University of Virginia; the focus of my studies was learning disabilities and social/emotional disorders. Although my special education degree is newly acquired, I am not a beginner. I have three years of experience as an elementary teacher. I have enclosed my resume, which provides details.

If it appears that my experience qualifies me for the position, I would appreciate a personal interview to discuss your needs and expand on my abilities in person.

Sincerely,

Christina Rivera

Sandra Swiercynski
200 E. Third Avenue
Lowell, MA 01854

March 13, 19 __

Marian Kelly
Kelly Career Consultants
1411 Main Street
Rockville, MD 20857

Dear Ms. Kelly:

I enjoyed meeting you last week at the NEVGA conference. Our conversation about your expanding private career consulting practice has stayed with me. As you know, I gave up my own private practice to direct the Campus Counseling Center at Lowell University. Although I enjoy my current position, the idea of returning to private practice is appealing. I would like to accept your offer to visit Rockville to discuss a possible position with your career consulting firm.

As an experienced counselor and former owner of my own practice, I can appreciate both the joys and difficulties of an expanding practice. I feel qualified to assist you with that overload because my client base has been large and diverse enough to include everything from college seniors struggling with career options to corporate clients seeking outplacement services for displaced workers.

My enclosed resume expands on my qualifications. What it doesn't adequately convey is the energy and strong sense of professionalism I bring to my work. I hope you still feel ready to hire an associate because I think our skills and personalities would mesh well.

I will call you next week to set up a meeting.

Sincerely,

Sandra Swiercynski

Thomas Luthra
33 Humphreys Street
Washington, DC 20059
(301) 555-8913--Home
(301) 555-5624--Business

May 14, 19___

Mr. David Rosenberg
American Federation for Academic Excellence
640 18th Street, NW
Washington, DC 20006

Dear Mr. Rosenberg:

I am enclosing my curriculum vitae in response to your May 10th advertisement in the *Washington Post*. I believe the credentials I would bring to the position of Director of Research will interest you. As my vitae indicates, I have extensive academic counseling expertise, management skills, and public relations ability gained at universities in the United States and abroad.

In my present position, as Director of the Career Planning Center at Howard University, I supervise a staff of nineteen and administer a career counseling and development program for Howard University students and faculty. I enjoy the challenge of providing prelaw counseling, designing career seminars, and assisting students with applications for graduate fellowships. Previously, I served the university for two years as Assistant Dean for Supportive Services. In that capacity I supervised a staff of seven, managed a budget of $840,000, and helped implement a university-wide tutoring program.

Page Two

My experience at Howard University is only a small part of my academic background. Details of my teaching and consulting experience (gained at Missouri Southern State College, Northeastern University, Tehran English Language Institute, and York College) are included in my vitae. The vitae also provides information about recent publications and awards.

As a professional educator I have the highest respect for the contributions your organization makes to the advancement of higher education in the United States. I would welcome the opportunity to assist in that effort as your new Director of Research. I look forward to hearing from you.

Sincerely,

Thomas Luthra

Theresa Porter
2453 Cambridge Road
Kansas City, MO 64108

June 24, 19__

Mr. Rahmell Jackson
Association of Midwest Nurses
6418 Tanglewood Lane
Kansas City, MO 64108

Dear Mr. Jackson:

I was excited to learn, via your announcement in the _American Library Journal,_ that the Association of Midwest Nurses is expanding its research library. After reviewing the enclosed resume, I hope that you will agree that I am highly qualified for the position of reference librarian at your facility.

Since receiving my MLS from Rosary College in 1986, I have worked for Wright High School and as a librarian for the Kansas City Public Libraries. My supervisors value my work and enthusiasm and have witnessed my skill in the following areas:

*Budget development   *Community outreach
*Materials acquisition   *Staff training and supervision

If you feel a personal interview is appropriate, I am available at your convenience. You may reach me at my home number 555-0654, or on a confidential basis at work, 555-6435. I am looking forward to your reply.

Respectfully,

Theresa Porter

Milton R. Rosenburg
650 Second Street
Portland, Oregon 97204
(503) 555-6418

February 2, 19__

Mr. David Elkin, Director
Cheney Community Center
750 Green Street
Tacoma, Washington 98447

Dear Mr. Elkin:

As social service professionals, we understand the devastating effect of substance abuse on our communities. In my work as a counselor at the Portland Mental Health Center, I face the challenge of assisting substance abusers every day. I would like to relocate to my Tacoma and am hoping there may be room on the staff at Cheney for a counselor with my expertise.

In addition to my counseling background, I have both a degree and experience in the field of leisure and recreation. I planned and created the Seattle Community Center in 1990 to provide guidance and supervised activities for local youth. Previous to that I was the Student Activities Director at Pacific Lutheran University in Tacoma.

If this combination of recreational and counseling skills seems a match for your current needs, you may reach me at (503) 555-6418 to discuss my qualifications further or arrange a personal interview.

Thank you for your consideration.

Yours truly,

Milton R. Rosenburg

Ann Olivera
664 E. Ivy Drive
Nashville, TN 37212

July 11, 19___

Ms. Indira Suresh
Adoption Services Coordinator
Belmont Child and Family Services
16 S. Belmont Road
Nashville, Tennessee 37212

Dear Ms. Suresh:

Your colleague, Martha Baylor, has encouraged me to write to you regarding a possible position at Belmont Child and Family Services as an adoptions caseworker. I currently work at Greater Nashville Social Service, where I supervise an adoptions intake unit with a staff of four. The enclosed resume explains my experience in the fields of adoption, child custody, verterans' affairs, psychiatric crisis intervention, and domestic violence.

Both my experience and client base have been diverse, which enables me to handle complex and emotionally charged social service cases with relative ease. My commitment to my profession is strong, as the references listed on my resume will attest. Continued education is essential in our work, and I strive to stay abreast of both legal issues and current theory on adoption. One of my strengths is my ability to empathize with all parties in adoption and custody cases and understand the needs and rights of both biological parents and adoptive families.

If I can provide further information about my credentials, please feel free to contact me at home (555-5412) or at work (555-8100). I would enjoy meeting with you at your convenience to discuss the fine work you do at Belmont.

Sincerely,

Ann Olivera

VGM CAREER BOOKS

VGM Career Horizons
a division of *NTC Publishing Group*
4255 West Touhy Avenue
Lincolnwood, Illinois 60646–1975